MAKE YOUR LIFE A MIRACLE

There are as many ways of praying as there are of living, yet the power of prayer to change lives is unique and constant, as this extraordinary collection of worldwide witness proves. Prayer that works speaks a universal language, and that voice of faith is represented here in personal testimony from all corners of the earth: from prominent educators, missionaries, clerics, philosophers, yogis, mystics, sages and saints.

The roads are varied, the possibilities limitless, and the options are **yours**—progress toward the greatest riches of all: meaningful prayer which yields life's highest possible dividends.

YES IT'S LOVE

Your Life Can Be A Miracle

Edited by
OREST BEDRIJ

E FAMILY LIBRARY   •   NEW YORK

YES IT'S LOVE
Your Life Can Be A Miracle

A FAMILY LIBRARY BOOK

First printing May, 1974

Copyright © 1974 by Orest Bedrij
All Rights Reserved

Library of Congress Catalog Card Number: 73-21089

ISBN: 0-515-03398-7

Printed in the United States of America

FAMILY LIBRARY is published by Pyramid Publications
919 Third Avenue, New York, New York 10022, U.S.A.

CONTENTS

DEDICATED TO YOU, MY LOVE

BE LIKE JESUS,
SO THAT YOU MAY ALWAYS
CALL HIM FATHER.

I would like to thank all the authors in this volume for lending their hand—and their ideas—in the preparation and completion of this collection.

And also many thanks to P. Curau, S. B. Lee, and G. Timpano, for much valuable help.

I extend my love and thanks to my beautiful wife, who made this book possible.

ACKNOWLEDGEMENTS

The authors wish to extend their thanks for permission to use copyrighted material from the following:

The New American Bible, copyright © 1970 by Confraternity of Christian Doctrine, The Catholic Press, Washington, D.C.

Today's English Version of the New Testament, copyright © 1966, 1967, American Bible Society. "Dimensions of Defensive Prayer."

From *Quarterly Journal of Spiritual Frontiers Fellowship* by T. N. Tiemeyer (Spiritual Frontiers Fellowship, Inc., Evanston, Illinois).

Ena Twigg: Medium by Ena Twigg with Ruth Hagy Brod (Hawthorn Books, Inc., New York, New York).

The Meaning of Prayer by the Archbishop of Canterbury (A. R. Mowbray & Co. Ltd., London, England).

Sermon on the Mount by Emmet Fox (Harper & Row, Publishers, New York, New York).

A NOTE TO THE READER

We have made no attempt to fit the authors into any particular theological mold. Each author writes from his own viewpoint, out of his own theological milieu.

The authors have contributed their articles independently of each other. Thus, the appearance of a particular work herein should not be construed as meaning that the author agrees with the theology, approach, or conclusions of any other author.

INTRODUCTION

This book can change your life.

If you are rich, poor, peasant, king, or whoever—you can change your destiny, shape events, perform miracles, heal the sick, become a creative giant, achieve a state of spiritual exaltation, attune your mind to the Creator of the Universe, and be what Socrates, Moses, Saint Paul, Newton, and thousands of other giants were.

The possibilities are limitless. The limitations are only what you make them. By applying the ideas of this book you can tap the mightiest Power in the Universe. This power is a source of all things that exist. It need only flow into your being and transform itself into health, inspiration, or anything else you may need or desire. You don't have to be unhappy; you don't have to live in fear or poverty. Your Father created a beautiful universe with all the riches you ever needed to use and enjoy. This power is everywhere. It belongs to all. It is waiting for you to apply it—not merely in crisis but for every occasion, every day of your life.

You will learn about the wisdom of the ages and the essence of the Bible and metaphysics. You will learn about the answer to our world problems. You will find that wars, atrocities, murder, poverty, human slavery, and misery can be eliminated.

By tapping the miracle Love of your Father, you can enjoy peace, love, radiant health, happiness, genius, unlimited knowledge—and much more. Literally you can bend the forces of nature to your will through prayer. You don't have to look for solutions. You have them within your grasp here, now. You can open the doors to life's most profound mysteries. This is not a pie-in-the-sky wish. This is reality. It works miracles.

Prayer has changed my life: it can change yours, too. Through prayer, I have found inner peace, happiness, and a real joy in living. Through prayer, you can find these same things.

When I began to share my thoughts on how to pray, I realized that I knew very little about prayer. In fact, I could share only what was "one man's opinion." Because I wanted people to experience what I had experienced, I knew that I had to ask others to help. Therefore, I asked prayerful people—clergymen and laymen—from many denominations, living in many lands, to share their thoughts.

These thoughts are collected here and presented in the hope that they will in some way prove useful to you.

As you go through these pages, you will find that there is no one perfect way to pray. There are many roads (and forms of prayer) that lead to the Creator. But whatever the road, you must embark and start traveling now. The sooner you realize this, the sooner will your life be what you want it to be.

You probably remember the story of a small boy and a wise old man:

"I have a bird in my hands," said the boy to the wise man. "Is it alive or is it dead?"

"I will trap him," thought the boy. "If he says it is dead I will let the bird fly away. But if he says it is alive I will crush the life out of it."

What is your answer? Will you start living to your fullest? Will you tap the Absolute Love and allow yourself to be what God wants you to be? You have every-thing to gain and nothing to lose. Do you want to help yourself? Do you want to help others? Test it, experi-ment, take notes and verify what Buddha, Mohammed, Pascal, Einstein, and millions of others have found: that prayer is too sacred and too powerful not to be given to the entire human race.

But back to the wise man, who smiled lovingly and said, "His life is in your hands." So is yours. You can be what your Father wanted you to be! Jesus tells us, "It is written in your own Law that God said 'You are gods.'" Then He added, "We know that what the scrip-ture says is true forever" (John 10:34-36). Which will it be? Will you be like the man who found a bag of diamonds while looking for sugar and threw it away because they failed to dissolve in his mouth? Or having found prayer, will you make your life a miracle?

Orest Bedrij

SUFFER THE LITTLE ONES

Samuel B. Lee

Praise, thanksgiving, forgiveness, and petition are our side of our conversation with God. In the silence of our hearts, notes Samuel B. Lee, God speaks to us and brings us the joy of His presence.

Samuel B. Lee is a graduate of the Catholic University of America. He is a professional writer who specializes in the area of technical publications. He has been active in the Confraternity of Christian Doctrine for many years. He is currently involved with the Charismatic Renewal and is a member of the Promise of Life Charismatic Community in Hopewell Junction, N.Y.

When I was very young, I was taught that prayer was the lifting of the mind and heart to God. And I was advised to pray always. So, I would try very hard, with eyes tightly shut, to lift my mind and heart to God. But I couldn't do this even for a little while. How, then, was I to pray always?

I soon became discouraged with prayer. True, I wanted to pray, I had been told how to pray, and yet I found I couldn't lift my mind and heart to God. And so my prayer life remained until I learned, many years later, that those old words, which I found so hard to

practice, contained the deepest truths about prayer. To
lift, or turn, one's mind and heart to someone is to communicate with him.

Put simply, prayer is conversation with God. And
like conversation, prayer is two-sided. We not only
speak to God, but we spend time in quiet so that God
can speak to us. And how do we speak to God? We
speak to Him as the father that He is.

Imagine a father and son playing catch with a baseball in the late fall. And imagine that they lose the ball
in the weeds. The father immediately promises to get
the boy a new ball in the spring. When spring comes,
the son simply reminds the father of the lost ball, and
the father's promise is made good. The important point
here is that the father's response—answering the son's
reminder—is based on the simple words of a son to a
father.

And so it must be between ourselves and our heavenly Father. We should talk to Him as the son in our little
episode undoubtedly spoke to his earthly father: re-
spectfully, in friendship and love, and with the expecta-
tion that he would get what he had been promised.

This is not to say that formal prayer has no place in
our prayer life. It has. And most of all we should pray
that perfect prayer to the Father taught us by His Son.
But we cannot be satisfied to limit ourselves to the set,
formal prayers we learned as children. We can no more
carry on all our conversations with God using set for-
mulas than business partners can talk over the problems
of their business using the ritualisms of cocktail party
small talk.

The ways of talking to God are as varied as the ways
of talking to our friends. But several threads run
through all prayer. These threads form the items of mutual interest between ourselves and our Father. They

appear most obviously in the prayer that Jesus taught us.

Two of these threads we can call adoration and thankfulness: "Blessed be your name . . . Your kingdom come . . . Your will be done . . . Father in Heaven . . ." Jesus shows us very clearly that we must bless and praise the Father, and through our praise and blessing show our thankfulness. Praise and thankfulness should form the bulk of our side of our conversations with God. And praise should be easy for us because we can turn nowhere without encountering Him in His creation: the beauty of His sunset; the coolness of His shade; His fire and hail, snow and frost, mountains and hills and all His mighty deeds.

We do not need formal prayers to thank our Father for giving us a spouse, a job, children, some measure of success, some small satisfaction in our work, warm days, cool nights, flowers, friends. We do not need formal prayers any more than we need a preset formula in order to thank a friend for a small birthday present. All we need to do is to say "Thank you" as it comes to us. Our friend understands; so does our Father.

Another thread is called forgiveness. "Forgive us our sins as we have forgiven those who have sinned against us . . ." And we are asked not only to forgive simply, but to forgive with that profoundness that includes completely forgetting the offense. We are called upon to put ourselves right with our friends so that no wall or wound stands between us.

After we have adored the Father and been thankful that He is God, and forgiven our fellow man, we can then weave the final thread—that of petition—into the tapestry of our prayer. "Give us this day . . . Lead us not . . . Deliver us from evil."

When I was young, I almost never thought of God

unless I needed something. Then it was easy to pray, at least for a little while. And I believe that most people turn to God only when they need something. Most of the time, He is like an insurance policy: nice to know it's around, but not really much good until you have an accident. Ah, then how important it suddenly becomes!

But our Father doesn't want to be merely an "insurance policy" God. He wants us to come to Him with thanks and praise, and not just with our petitions. He wants to be more like the car—used every day—than the insurance policy—used only "in emergency." Besides, God knows our needs better than we do. Our earthly fathers knew when we needed new shoes, a schoolbook, or a coat; how much more our heavenly Father knows our needs. If we could truly seek the kingdom of heaven by praising, thanking, and forgiving, we would have, I think, very little need to ask our Father for anything. He would supply it before even we knew we needed it.

Our conversation with God—praise, thanksgiving, forgiveness, and petition—should be like human conversation: Each person speaks, and each listens; and each can enjoy the silent companionship of the other.

God's ways of speaking to us are not our ways. He does not always speak as a voice that we hear. He may speak to us by giving us a new insight into His word as we read it; or He may speak to us through something someone says to us. But most frequently, our Father speaks to us in the silence of our hearts as we come near to Him and silently enjoy being in His presence.

And this is the joy of prayer —to be in the presence of God and know that He loves us, protects us, and guides us. That we can speak to Him who keeps the stars in place and know that He hears us. That we can speak to God, and know that He answers us.

THE PRAYER FACTOR

Marcus Bach

In this selection, Dr. Marcus Bach draws upon his knowledge of religions from around the world. He finds that from the diversity of kinds of prayers emerges a common experience: the elevation to and beyond the moral.

Dr. Bach is a world traveler, author, and popular interpreter of intercultural relations. *Who's Who* lists him as the foremost authority on contemporary religious movements and analyst of the American scene. He holds a Ph.D from the University of Iowa and four honorary degrees from other universities; he has been recognized with numerous awards, has authored twenty books, has written numerous articles for national periodicals, and has served as a specialist in the Department of State under the International Educational Exchange program in Southeast Asia, India, Pakistan, Korea and Japan. Dr. Bach is a founder and director of the Fellowship for Spiritual Understanding, Palos Verdes, California.

Have you ever wondered what people think of when they pray? What do they concentrate on, what frame of mind are they in, what happens when they pray?

I have asked these questions of worshipers in many faiths.

One said, "I fix my mind on thankfulness. Gratitude for my blessings is the key to prayer."

Another told me, "I visualize God as the highest and greatest love imaginable and I see my life as part of that love. I kneel when I pray. I close my eyes and shut out all worldly thoughts. I think of God as a great spiritual Father who created all and who governs all. Then I listen for His voice. His voice comes to me in the form of thoughts and impressions. I actually talk to Him and He talks to me."

Others have confided in me:

"I put all my troubles and problems aside and begin by saying, 'God, I want only to worship Thee.' I keep repeating this until there is no other thought in my mind than this."

"I think of the beauty of nature. I can pray best out of doors, where I feel the fellowship with God."

"I mentally enter a golden tunnel. God is at the far end in a dazzling light. I go farther and farther toward the light until my consciousness merges with His."

"I sit Yoga fashion when I pray. I breathe regularly and say, 'God is my light, God is my life.' I do not ask for anything or expect anything. I just fill myself with the thought that my life is God's life."

"I think of goodness and peace and try to fill my spirit with them."

"I visualize two chambers—one spaceless and eternal, the chamber of God, the Father. The other contains all created things and is ruled over by Christ. I walk through these chambers led by the power of the Holy Spirit. That is how I pray."

"When I pray I make my mind completely receptive to whatever God wants me to know."

"When I pray I mentally hear Jesus saying, 'Come unto Me.'"

"Prayer for me is just being still and feeling God's presence."

All of these worshipers had found something; all were still seeking something.

The secret, of course, is to start with ourselves. Someone may intercede for you or pray for you, but no one can truly "find God" for you. It is an inner experience.

You must begin with yourself and develop the inward look.

You must take time for meditation and prayer.

Life is the laboratory. Life is the heart of faith. Life is the great adventure.

You must give God *His* minute. *His* ten minutes. *His* hour. There is no other way. There is no greater secret. *You* are the one who must begin. *You* are the person that matters. *You* in your own faith, whatever the faith may be, *you* are the person to whom God will reveal Himself if you but take time to worship Him.

Right now, if you close your eyes for a moment and think of God—no matter how vague your concept of Him may be—you have already begun an adventure in faith.

An American businessman said to me, "We should not entreat God or force God or beg of God. We should simply become aware in body, mind, and spirit that we are possessed by God fully and completely."

He said that when he first set aside a few moments for prayer in his office, his mind was clouded by a rush of thoughts having to do with business, appointments, and problems for the day. His biggest problem was to "keep God in focus." He soon learned that each time he brought his thoughts back to concentrate on the thought of God, the thought grew stronger. Each time he warded off worldly thoughts, God became clearer.

I have learned this from many religions around the world. "When you start thinking about the Lord, the Lord starts thinking about you" is the way a Moslem put it.

When the period of meditation or prayer is finished, God should remain as a lingering Presence.

When you open your eyes and look upon the world, you should do so with a new inner vision. You are not alone, say those who worship, you are never alone. God and you are one.

An instructor in Yoga told me, "If the spiritual exercises leave you exhausted, you are not doing them correctly. They should leave you calm and refreshed."

That is also true of prayer. If your excursion into the "silence" leaves you disquieted or disturbed, you are not worshiping correctly. You have merely sought an escape. Worship and prayer are "finding God" and God is always goodness, peace, and strength.

The "quiet time" or period of meditation, wherever it is sincerely practiced, always develops a feeling of the authority of the moral in God. That is, the immoral becomes opposition to God. The better the worship, the better the man; and, conversely, the better the man, the better the worship.

It is an adventure, a quest.

A person may be moral without any specific religious discipline, but he cannot be religious without advancing in morality. Worship always leads beyond the moral. It persuades the worshiper to be critical of himself and to try to be a better person than he was before he worshiped.

JOURNEY TO THE SACRED SELF

Yogi Amrit Desai

How can we find peace, love, and contentment in this harried world? Yogi Amrit Desai affirms that we must turn within and, through prayer and effort, begin the journey of self-realization that is union with God.

Yogi Desai is a close disciple of the great Yogi Guru Swami Kripalvanandji. He is the founder and director of the Yoga Society of Pennsylvania and has recently established Kripalu Ashram-Retreat near Philadelphia, where he lives. Besides his abilities as a teacher, lecturer, and writer, Yogi Desai has a B.F.A. degree and is a recognized artist. His work in the fields of Yoga and the arts has brought him many honors and awards.

The Journey Within

Often a man caught up in a hurricane of worldly life, in spite of all earthly efforts, finds himself pushed around helplessly, like a straw, in utter confusion and darkness, leading him to search the infinite power of the Divine. Thus, a man tempered by time and experience humbles himself and accepts the higher self, the divine father, as his saviour. He then has the fuel of faith to start his journey within. His spontaneous cries for help under these circumstances are always answered, because they fulfill all the necessary conditions for true prayer. Some are led within only when they experience great suffering in life, while others are led within for the love toward the divine father within.

Prayer

Prayer is the most effective means to start the journey within. The purpose of prayer is to establish communication with God, the father within—to receive guidance, wisdom, and strength to tread the path of self-realization. For prayers to be effective, one must fulfill the necessary conditions. Sometimes such conditions are spontaneously fulfilled, but sometimes man has to prepare his life to bring about right conditions for communication within. All prayers must be accompanied by the corresponding effort. The effort and prayer complement each other like a chariot with two wheels. Prayer without effort is like a chariot with one wheel. A great Indian, Yogi Ramakrishna, says, "The wind of God's grace is always blowing but we have to put up our sails." It is also said that God helps those who help themselves. This shows that God is everywhere, and that means within us as well. Thus, God works through us but not for us.

In the popular approach, only verbal prayers are offered to God in heaven. But great Yogis and Masters say that God is within us. Yogis say, "Tat Twam Asi," thou art that; "Sohum," I am that. Jesus says, "The kingdom of heaven is within," and he also says, "Know thyself." If God is omnipresent, omniscient, and omnipotent, he is within us too. Thus, there is nothing within us that is secret to God. Every thought or action, no matter how secretly or unconsciously performed, is known to the higher self within and has its effect on future actions automatically. This is why verbal, mechanical, ceremonial prayers fail. This is why successful prayer does not depend on careful selection or arrangement of words; such prayers are merely lip service.

Since true prayer is two-way communication with God, verbal prayer should be followed by a silent conscious period. (Conscious verbal prayer without the silent period is like one-way talk, which cannot be called communication.) For successful communication, conscious verbal prayer should lead to silent listening prayer. This listening prayer is called meditation. Listening becomes possible when the mind becomes empty and still. As long as the mind is striving, expecting, interpreting, or asking, it cannot be empty. In listening prayer, which is far more superior, man opens gates to the divine inner guidance by placing himself in a state of holy indifference or choiceless awareness and surrendering to the will of the divine. In conscious verbal prayers of petition, praise, supplication, or adoration, man uses his conscious mind, which censors thoughts and feelings according to its own conditioning. In verbal prayers man talks to God, but in listening prayers God talks to man. At this point, through surrender, man becomes one with God. Thus, meditation is a royal path (Raja Yoga) to God.

Our Whole Life Should Become a Prayer

Thus, true prayers are offered not only by our words but also by our most secret thoughts and actions. Under these circumstances, all our desires, expressions, and actions, conscious or unconscious, become our prayers.

This is why one must purify one's thoughts, words, and actions to pray. Also, one should pray, at the same time, to receive inner strength and guidance to purify. Thus, prayer and purity quickly pave the path to progress and the divine. Thus, one must pray with one's whole life. The incongruency in one's thoughts, words, and actions is a basic impurity, and this in turn brings fear, tensions, and imbalance. This blocks the inflow of the universal energy and separates man from the universal orchestra of harmony and unity, leading him further and deeper into disharmony.

To bridge the individual self with the universal self, one must vibrate with the laws of the universe. To accomplish this, man must act in the right direction with all available wisdom, energy, logic, and reasoning, along with prayers. If we consider our verbal prayers as a seed suggestion for our future, our actions are the supersuggestion that supersedes all other prayers. Thus, prayer is a continuous, spontaneous, effortless flow expressed through our mental, emotional, verbal, and physical actions. Any prayers not coming through our whole being are not answered. This is why we hear the popular expression "Deserve before you demand."

Faith—Surrender

Without faith one cannot truly pray or pursue the higher path with patience. Faith is the fuel that sustains actions in the right direction without distractions. A great yogi of India, Swami Kripalvanandji, says, "A man of faith continues his efforts in one direction with patience for many years, while a man without faith changes many directions in a day." Thus, prayers without faith fail to bear fruit.

Faith means firm inner conviction in the divine self. God within is a sole source of truth consciousness and bliss. This conviction coordinates and focuses all mental, emotional, and physical energies in a singleness of purpose to reach the paramount source of light. With this kind of faith, one naturally and effortlessly, renounces all attachments of body, ego, and mind, which represent the lower self. Without such faith there is no way to surrender one's lower self into the hands of the higher self.

To surrender means to surrender all the ego-oriented selfish actions to the divine within and say, "Thy will be done, not mine." As this surrender matures with prayers supported by efforts, one rises above personal insecurities, fears, confusion, and tension. To the extent one surrenders, one begins to see the guiding and comforting light within. This starts the journey toward the heaven within. The surrender lifts man above the narrow, limited, conditioned self and places him in touch with the unlimited source of energy and peace within. He wants nothing for his lower self and becomes merely an instrument or channel of the divine. In such total surrender he lives, moves, and acts in and for divine will. Thus, he emerges from the world of duality, polarity, and contrasts; they exist only for the person whose lower self is active and who says, "My will be done, not thine." He is a prodigal son who suffers. When the prodigal starts his journey back home to meet his father with faith and surrender, he feels increasingly contented and at peace within. This is not an ordinary peace but, as Christ says, "Peace that passeth all understanding." Finally when man gives up all his ego-oriented desires and lives fully by the will of his father, his individuality merges with cosmic consciousness. This union in

Sanskrit is called Yoga, which results in Samadhi. This mystical union is the direct experience. *"I and my father are one."*

WHAT IS PRAYER?

Sister Cecile Sandra

Prayer, asserts Sister Cecile Sandra, is the enriching intercommunication between God and men. When undertaken with an open heart and an open mind, it becomes the liberating experience that unites mankind.

Sister Cecile Sandra, I.C.M., O.B.E., Ph.D., received her doctorate in psychology from Fordham University and is now a member of the Religious Congregation of the Missionary Sisters of the Immaculate Heart of Mary with headquarters in Rome. She has been engaged in school administration and lecturing in psychology in the Caribbean since 1956 and is presently on the staff of St. Michael's Seminary in Kingston, Jamaica. Sister Cecile Sandra is a member of numerous education and mental health associations in the United States as well as the Caribbean.

Prayer is communication with God and all his people.

Is there any set formula for such communication? There hardly could be any, since communication occurs according to each person's own unique personality. It is with this personality that we have to discover and rediscover our personal God day by day. We discover Him in myriad ways: in the slender palm tree along the winding mountain road, in the angry sea beating the eroding stacks, in the translucent rainbow on a clearing sky, in the "blue light" foreshadowing the daily death of the sun.

We discover Him and, with a touch of His divinity, we are ready to meet men again and find in them another touch of the divine and blend it all in one enriching and refreshing intercommunication.

If we remain attuned to the divine in ourselves and others, we will find God in the sounds all around: in the promising cry of the twins next door, in the dreamy steelband at nighttime, and in the lively guitar chords of the youngsters in church—and—hosannah—have mercy—be merry—let's be proud of the band. We will find Him anew, and thus enriched, we will be able to meet others and enter into that process of mutual enrichment—of true humanization with God ever in the picture.

If we keep our affinity for the divine in our lives, we will see God in the many faces of humanity today: in the charismatic hands of the religious leader, in the restless head of the young radical, in the dynamic smile of the newlywed, in the motionless gaze of the old Grannie, and in the hungry look of the kid on his way to the tap at the street corner.

We will meet the Lord and this encounter will stimulate other encounters and lift up humanity while enriching us.

God has many faces in the 1970's. To me His face is one of liberation.

"God, free me," says the young man in the affluent home. Free me! From what? From the deadening comfort, the sophisticated smiles, the artifacts and the taboos all around me. Free me from role-playing, from enforced acting, from deadening compulsion, from the obsession that I'll never make the grade for the twenty-first century. Free my better self and open it up for You and for others. God, liberate me! God, liberate us, say the young people in the developing countries. We have joined hands, God, because we remain in want, even though the "first world" has it all in abundance. We can't be free if we remain oppressed, Lord!

God, help us to grow to the stature of the others. If only they could liberate us of our dependency on them.

God, why don't the wealthy nations realize that You want them—not as individuals, but as groups? Help us to discover our inner wealth and that of our culture and that of our people everywhere—in what they love to call "The third world."

God, our God, we will discover You fully when they let us grow, when they believe that we too, Your people, have the potential to enrich others because we have suffered more and have been freed from self in the process and will know how to communicate with all others in a positive way, if only they are great enough to meet us with an open mind and an open heart.

UNION WITHOUT CEASING

OREST BEDRIJ

Orest Bedrij has found among Jesus, the apostles and saints, scholars and seers, guidance in achieving the prayer life of union with God through love.

Bedrij, a native of Ukraine, received his education in electrical engineering and finance in the United States. Professionally he has been involved in the computer sciences and has been the technical director of the California Institute of Technology Jet Propulsion Laboratory, Space Flight Facility. He is president and director of Securities Council and founder of a number of computer corporations.

The world now needs prayer more than any other thing. For ages man has been trying to find solutions to war, genocide, atrocity, poverty, slavery, murder, drunkenness, drug addiction, immorality, riots and lynchings, sickness, and on . . . and on . . . and on.

Have we been successful? Have we come close to the real answer? No, because we have not been using the right tool: we have not been using prayer, the master key to life that our Father has put in our hands. Prayer

---

Biblical references in italics are from the *New American Bible;* others are from *Good News For Modern Man.*—EDITOR

can conquer all problems. Study the history of man's intercession with His Creator and you will find that when properly asked, your Father will give you whatever you need. All you have to do is ask in Jesus' name and He will provide.

God created you and the universe, with its immensity of splendor and beauty, for you to use and enjoy. Certainly he can help you with your problems. He is waiting and longing to give you much more than the cup you hold up to be filled. But you have to turn to Him. Nobody can do it for you. You have to do it yourself. "He has knocked at the door" (Rev 3:20). And you have to open the door of your heart and let Him in.

You can read about prayer. You can talk about prayer. You can listen to beautiful sermons. You can attend conferences or help with bazaars. But "let those men of zeal," recommended St. John of the Cross, "who think by their preaching and exterior works to convert the world, consider that they would be much more pleasing to God—to say nothing of the example they give—if they would spend at least one half of their time in prayer." Some later time, perhaps tomorrow, perhaps next year you will take the next step of prayer. But not now. Now is not the right time. You want the gifts of God without paying the price. Which will it be for you? Will you get involved? Will you do it now? The choice is clearly yours. And the proof is in praying —constantly praying with your heart and your mind and your whole being. You will stop believing in God; you will start seeing Him! You will be consciously walking in Him. He will be your guiding light, your shining perfection, your strength, your courage, and your wisdom. *You will really feel that He dwells in you and you in Him.* Every moment will be His moment. You will drink His life. You will drink His love. You will lose yourself in Him. You and He will be one. You will cry out with a loud voice of Christ: "Eli, Eli, lmana shabachthani! which means, My God, My God, this was my destiny. I was born for this" (Matt 27:46).*

Here is a list of points you will find helpful as you grow in your prayer life:

1. Make prayer a definite part of each day.
2. Find a quiet place.
3. Be comfortable.
4. Be attentive.
5. Ask God to teach you how to pray.
6. Know yourself.
7. Thank God frequently.
8. Pray with your heart.
9. Fast.
10. Have faith.
11. Be still.

Let's look at each one of these and see how they help you attain the union without ceasing that has been called by Dr. R. M. Bucke "cosmic consciousness," by Christian mystics "unitive life" or "beatific vision," by Buddhists "Nirvana," and by Hindus "Moksha."

1. *Make prayer a definite part of each day.* Set aside a certain time each day, the earlier the better. In the beginning make it five minutes, ten minutes, or whatever your busy schedule permits. Remember: the less you pray, the less you want to pray. No one ever learned how to fly in one easy lesson. It takes time and effort. The great pianist and composer Rachmaninoff said that when he skipped one day's practice he knew it, when he

---

The Gospel Light, Comments on the Teachings of Jesus from Aramaic and Unchanged Eastern Customs, by George Lansa Copyright © 1936, 1939, renewed © 1964 by A. J. Holman Co. Reprinted by permission of A. J. Holman Co., a division of J. B. Lippincott Co.

skipped two days' practice the critics knew it, and after three days, the audience knew it. This is even truer with prayer. Every lapse is a setback and joy lost forever. The goal is to learn to pray always, in all places, without interruption.

2. *Find a quiet place*—any place, outside or inside: an empty room, an attic, a church, a park, a garden, a lakeside bench, a mountain, a bathroom, or a closet. Be certain you will not be disturbed. True, you can pray while scrubbing pots and pans in the kitchen or while driving or on the train. However, the deeper experiences of prayer come in solitude. Jesus advises, "Whenever you pray, go to your room, close your door, and pray to your Father in private. Then your Father, who sees what no man sees, will repay you" (*Matt* 6:6).

3. *Be comfortable.* Traditionally Westerners kneel, because kneeling happens to be the accepted gesture of respect before an earthly throne. We know from Matthew that Jesus "threw himself face down to the ground and prayed fervently" (Matt 26:39). Easterners seem to feel that sitting erect with spine straight and the body in equipoise, is most conducive to prayer. Possibly there is no "right" posture. You have to pray in the position that suits you best. It's not the position of your body but the state of your heart that counts.

4. *Be attentive.* Keep your mind fixed on Him. To do this, you should not be overtired, torpid, overfed, or sleepy. Your body should be tranquil and free from physical and mental tensions. The Swedes have a beautiful proverb which may be used as a guide: "Fear less, hope more; eat less, chew more; whine less, breathe more; talk less, say more; hate less, love more; and all good things are yours."

5. *Ask God to teach you how to pray.* If you think

you know how to pray, listen to Saint Teresa: "Those who walk in the way of prayer have the greater need of learning; and the more spiritual they are, the greater is their need."

No matter what you have heard, or read, prayer is no simple task. And it is impossible to pray properly without His help. "Prayer is the hardest kind of work," confesses space scientist Dr. Werner Von Braun, "but it is the most important work we can do now." "Here I am, God," tell Him. "Without your help I'm sunk. Holy Spirit, take my weakness, enlighten me, and guide me into all truth." (And He will!) Let Him fill your heart and mind and kindle in you the fire of His love. Let Him make you complete—an overwhelming experience of beauty, love, and joy. Let Him bring you into the exhilarating experience of the presence of God.

6. *Know yourself.* Purify your soul and put your life in order. Search your heart for the sins you have made in thought and deed that have hurt others, as well as yourself. Realize that your sins and failures prevent God's love from working in your life, and unless you remove all barriers, the free flow of His love will be blocked. Jesus recommended, "If you bring your gift to the altar and there recall that your brother has anything against you, leave your gift at the altar, go first to be reconciled, and then come back and offer your gift" (*Matt* 5:23, 24). No trespass should be too great for you to forgive. Hanging on the Cross, the Light of Life prayed for those who were killing him: "Father, forgive them; they do not know what they are doing" (*Luke* 23:34). A forgiving spirit toward others is required for effective prayer and your own health, and God will forgive you only in the measure in which you forgive. So be merciful—and set yourself free.

Often we are our own debtor. We have trespassed. We have to ask His forgiveness. Tell Him with the heart of a child in humility and sorrow: "O Father, I am sorry! Forgive me!" And He will forgive you and forget. His forgiveness is the love that completely burns out the past sins. You then have to forgive yourself— not partially but completely. You must not recount over and over your wrongdoing. Bury the garbage of past mistakes, otherwise it is spiritual suicide. It's like opening a wound that is once clean. You will make it septic again. Having confessed, turn your back upon your transgressions and be ready in the future to "hate the sin," as the jail inscription at Karnal-India advises, but "not the sinner." Then, "Avoid all evil, cherish all goodness," recommended Buddha, and "keep the mind pure." For, as Paul noted, you "are the temple of the living God" (2 *Cor* 6:16). And being holy is not only limited to deeds but also to thoughts. Jesus made this clear concerning adultery: "Anyone who looks lustfully at a woman has already committed adultery with her in his thoughts" (*Matt* 5:28).

All day long thoughts that occupy your mind are molding your destiny for good or evil. Once in a vision I saw a good and a bad thought. Chills ran up and down my spine when I realized their great power and the boomerang effect they have. Every thought, I realized then, is a high-frequency energy field that, if viewed with a suitable apparatus, would appear as real as an object you see. Nikola Tesla, for example, who invented the a/c motor, transformer, radar, fluorescent light, wireless remote control and so forth, could always see his thoughts. They were so vivid and full of solidity that at times it was difficult for him to distinguish between his thought and external reality. While looking at the image, he would construct many desired pieces of machinery completely in every detail and dimension. Sometimes he would test them—still in his mind—over a period of more than a year, observing the parts as they wore, modifying them, as needed.

If you could see your thoughts and their effect on your surrounding, you would literally be petrified to dwell on anything negative. You would realize that *the whole of your life's experience is but the outer expression of inner thoughts you have chosen to hold.* You would understand that what you think in your mind you will invariably produce in your experience. Think love, and the love energy emanating from your mind will not only surround and modify you but all those about whom you think. Think thoughts of hate, and hate energy will be acting on you and on those about whom you think.

Dr. William Parker demonstrated in the laboratory that if you hold a feeling of hard implacability against life or impulse of unkindness or jealousy, or anger, or hatred (love in reverse) toward someone, you are really slowly killing yourself. It's like grabbing a hot iron to hit someone but in fact hurting yourself instead. The Man of Galilee summarized it very beautifully: "Whatsoever you sow" in your unseen thoughts "that shall you also reap" in that which is seen. Illnesses (cancer, ulcers, heart attacks, and so on), murder, poverty (the list is endless) are self-inflicted thoughts. You have to change the prevailing tenor of your life on Love and you will see no darkness. For if you will not take the road of Light you will have to keep on learning by pain. Man cannot break the laws of God; he can only break himself against them. Only by much searching and mining will gold and diamonds be obtained. Therefore concentrate on the right choice and true application of God-like thoughts and deeds and you will grow through love to Love.

So with every breath, with every thought, with every aim, let love be love in you.

7. *Thank God frequently,* joyfully, and eagerly. Thank Him with the deepest affection of your heart for letting you be alive and part of His creation. Praise His goodness and love for you. Recall the many graces of mercy, happiness, joy, wisdom, ability, health He has given you; the many sins He has forgiven you; your ability to see His glory and drink from the spring of His Spirit. Thank Him always for everything that happens to you during every moment of your life.

"We don't thank God enough for much that He has given us," confesses Robert Woods, "our prayers are too often the beggar's prayer, the prayer that asks for something. We offer too few prayers of thanksgiving and praise."

Remember when Jesus healed the ten lepers? Why did only one return to give thanks to God? Were not ten cleansed (*Luke* 17:14-19)?

"When I look at your heavens," cried David, which "the work of thy fingers, the moon and the stars you have established; what is man that thou art mindful of him?" We are so small, our life so short, our knowledge so limited, we begin to feel with Tennyson that the life of men is but "murmur of gnats in the gleam of a million suns." Thank Him, adore Him because "Thou has made us for Thyself," sings St. Augustine, "and our hearts can find no rest outside of Thee." Ps 8:4

8. *Pray with your heart.* When you pray realize that you are addressing the Maker of all. He is the Love of loves, the Creator who is infinitely bigger to our universe than the universe is to an atom. The Absolute Beauty, Gentleness, Wisdom, Goodness, and Power. Do not address Him while you are thinking of other things.

Show your gratitude to Him for allowing you to come near Him. Remember, before you can really pray with sincerity you must begin to know the greatness and Holiness of God. And the greater the depth and extent of the knowledge, the more love there will be. The more easily the heart will soften and lay itself open to the love of God.

God knows before you open your lips what you will say. You must pray with your mind, your heart, and your whole life. You must seek to know His will, be eager to offer yourself to Him, and be ready to be filled with His Holy Spirit. You must pray in your own words, just the way you talk to friends. The cry from the heart of the most illiterate is just as welcome to God as the perfectly formed prayer of a great scholar. But it is not the utterances of the lips that God hears; rather the song and joy of the heart. If your heart does not speak, you are silent to God. Love God and He will hear you.

9. *Fast.* Deliberately abstain from food for spiritual purposes. Why fast? Isn't a good life adequate? Why did Jesus fast? Why did Moses, Samuel, David, Elijah, Daniel, Isaiah, Cornelius, Paul, Socrates, Plato, Buddha, Gandhi, Pythagoras, Luther, Lincoln . . . fast? Did they know something we don't know? Christ did not have to fast! He is the Light of Life and Perfection. Yet he taught, fasted, performed miracles, was crucified, died, and arose not for exhibition but to teach us how to grow. In his Sermon on the Mount Jesus did not say *"if* you pray . . . *if* you fast . . . *if* you give alms" but *"when* you pray . . . *when* you fast . . . *when* you give alms." His language for prayer and fast is identical. He expects us unambiguously, and without qualification, to pray, to fast, and to give when the occasion demands it. There is one requirement, however: when you fast, please God and not the eyes of other people. "Appear not to

men that you are fasting, but to your Father who is unseen: and your Father, who sees what is hidden will reward you" (Matt 6:18). The shameful hypocrisy, the egocentric piety, and showy acts of fasting of the Pharisees had no place in Jesus' life and must be curbed in your life. Fasting should be inconspicuous, noncompetitive, and uninjurious to your health. One to three days' fast is easy and does not fall into this category. But if you embark on a longer fast (7–40 days) be sure that God is leading you to do this and that you understand how to go about it. If you have an illness or doubts as to the physical advisability of fasting, consult your own doctor and follow his advice. (For additional reading we have listed some of the books you may consider.) Then why are you afraid to fast? Why are you not doing what Jesus has instructed you to do? Very simply: the evil spirits (earthbound, unenlightened, without God individuals) that Christ had to deal with are working against you. Every opportunity the Dark Forces get, every road block they can set up (chaos, disruption, fear, hatred, worry, aggression, separativeness) goes into action. In itself fasting has nothing of goodness or holiness, nor is it the true food or nourishment. But it clears the doors of perception and removes the impediments of holiness. It helps to crucify the self-love and self-will and allows God's overwhelming power to shape the real eternal you. It breaks down that which stands between God and you and *tunes your mind and body to be a better instrument for love.*

Both the Old and the New Testament very clearly state (74 times) that prayer and fasting are a must, that "man cannot live by bread alone, (Matt 4:4)" that some evil spirits can only be driven out by prayer and fasting (*Matt* 17:21). People who have fasted will testify that it constitutes one of the most powerful tools

God has put in your hands. When you fast you bring
a note of urgency to your prayer. You are telling God
that you are truly in earnest, that you do not intend to
take no for an answer, that you want a miracle.

The great prophet Isaiah (740–700 B.C.), who vividly
foretold the suffering and death of Jesus, listed some of
the benefits of fasting: answer to prayer, health, guidance, healing, inspiration, and the Glory of the Lord
shall be your reward (58:1-14). Can you wish for
more? Individuals who fast claim many other benefits:
Daniel—improvement of his prophetic ability; Elijah—
spiritual direction; Socrates, Plato, Plutarch, Pythagoras, and Galileo—sharpening of intellect and mental
clarity; the people of Israel—divine intervention; the
apostles—spiritual enrichment; Krishna, Buddha, Shan-
kara, Confucius, Gandhi—understanding of Truth; the
8,000 (1948 through the present) patients under Dr.
Yurij Nikolayev at Moscow's Gannushkin Institute—
treatment of sluggish forms of schizophrenia. The famous physical fitness authority Dr. Paul Bragg testifies
that "you purify your body physically, mentally, and
spiritually and therefore enjoy super vitality and super
health. Greatest of all are the inner peacefulness and
tranquillity that make life worth living. You come into
harmony with that Power higher than yourself. You
learn the meaning of the truth that 'your body is the
temple of the Living God.' " How to start? Very simply:
A. You have to believe that fasting is good for you.
B. If this is your first, don't start on a long fast. Learn
   to walk before you run.
C. Have fruit for your last meal.
D. Abstain completely (initially for 24 hours) from
   eating and drinking everything except water.
E. Drink as much boiled warm water as you wish.
F. The first time you fast you might get a headache,

especially if you are used to drinking coffee, tea, or alcohol. This is one of the signs that you are being depoisoned. It is unpleasant but good for you. You might consider stopping coffee, tea, or alcohol a few days before the fast.

G. To fight discouragement (evil spirit attacks) praise God.

H. Break fast with fruit or vegetable juices (apple, tomato, or citrus).

I. At the following mealtime have fresh salad (without dressing) or homemade vegetable soup (no fat). Avoid pastries, biscuits and starchy foods.

J. At first sensation of fullness stop eating.

K. To avoid pain and discomfort after a longer fast, Dr. Herbert Shelton (who has supervised over 30,000 healing fasts) advises that after the fast you discipline yourself and control your appetite and food intake.

10. *Have faith* that God will solve your problems. Realize that all things come from Him out of His love for us. "Ask, and you will receive," recommended the Man of Nazareth. "Seek, and you will find. Knock, and it will be opened to you. For the one who asks, receives. The one who seeks, finds. The one who knocks, enters" (*Matt* 7:7–8). Jesus' words assure that the door is wide open to receive whatsoever you desire for yourself or your loved ones. Just lay before Him the needs of your soul and body *believing that you have already received*. Open your heart reverently and wholeheartedly and He will bestow the richest blessing. "Would one of you hand his son a stone when he asks for a loaf, or a poisonous snake when he asks for a fish?" further teaches Jesus. "If you, with all your sins, know how to give your children what is good, how much more will your

Heavenly Father give good things to anyone who asks
Him" (*Matt* 7:9–11).

Your Father, the Ultimate Spring of Living Water,
is longing to help you with your needs. Therefore, *be
always alert and attuned to Him for inner guidance,
direction and support*. But once you know what has to
be done, you have to get up and do it. Suppose your
house were in darkness, yet there is a power line directly outside. All you have to do is bring that electric
line into your home. You have a choice: You can curse
the darkness or you can link the Eternal Light into your
life. However, if you assume that the purpose of prayer
is only to get what you want in material things from
God, then you may never rise far. There is a deeper
purpose and meaning to prayer. Pray with humility for
spiritual strength, help in avoiding sin, guidance, wisdom, understanding, and love. Pray for others, and
hold them up into the light of God's presence.

"There is nothing that makes us love a man so much
as praying for him," confesses William Law. "By considering yourself as an advocate with God for your
neighbors and acquaintances, you would never cease to
be at peace with them yourself . . . such prayers as these
amongst neighbors and acquaintances would unite them
to one another in the strongest bonds of love and tender-
ness."

Pray for those who hate you, pray for those who
persecute you. . . . Pray, love, and serve men in utter
selflessness. Be a channel through which Jesus may act.
We do not live alone, and we do not die alone. "We
are members of one another" (*Ephes* 4:25); "I am the
vine, you are the branches" (*John* 15:5), taught the
Light of Life. *Everything we say or do has some influence on everyone in the human community*.

The best petition is not to reach out in your own way

for what you don't understand completely but to leave
yourself in the arms of your Father and *let His will be
your will.* Let His law be your law. Let "not I, but Christ
in me" be your motto. Remember, when Jesus prayed
in the garden of Gethsemane he asked to be relieved
of the cross—"Abba [oh Father], you have the power to
do all things. Take this cup away from me. But *let it be
as you would have it, not as I*" (*Mark* 14:36).

11. *Be still,* and listen to God within. If you were
with a king or a president, would you be talking all the
time? Would you be asking without stopping—especially if the ruler could read your mind and know your
heart's desires before you opened your lips? "Your
Father," says Jesus, "knows what you need before you
ask Him" (*Matt* 6:8). Having done your talking and
petitioning, wait before Him in love, joy, adoration,
and devotion and listen to Him.

God speaks to your heart in silence. Silence means
more than ceasing to speak with your lips; it means
also practicing and *maintaining stillness in your mind*
(when you turn within, leave the problem outside).
Sometimes when you are praying, you may not speak
at all with your lips, but your mind is boiling over with
emotions and fears so that you cannot hear the "still
small voice" of God within you.

Dom John Chapman captured the essence of silence
when he stated that "you can't make silence—you can
make noise. But you can only make silence by stopping
the noise." The prophet Habakkuk testified: "But the
Lord is in his holy temple: let all the earth keep silence
before Him" (2:20). We should not let our cries for our
earthly needs disturb the inner peace of God's temple.
"A man does not see himself in running water," con-
firmed the sage Chuang Tzu, "but in still water." So,
make the stillness your own. Turn your creative facul-

ties into a receiving station and start listening not only with your ears but with your entire being to the still small voice of God's whisper. As you listen and rest in His love you may come to feel as though the whole world were vibrating with the Presence and Love of God, with absolute peace and stillness and yet with an intense and ceaseless energy. *IN THIS STILLNESS YOU WILL LEARN WHO YOU REALLY ARE.* You will learn of love. You will learn of patience, humility, peace, joy, and life. You will learn of Him. This learning you have to do yourself. No book or teacher can tell you the feeling of quietness, clearness, stillness, love, or beauty. You have to experience it yourself. There is no other way. The teacher can show you the direction, but you have to throw your whole self into the journey. You have to "be still and know that I am God" (*Ps* 46:11).

An unknown writer described "wait still upon God. Open your heart to Him, let the light and warmth of His love flood your mind and heart and soul as silently as the flower opens itself to, and drinks in, the light and warmth of the sun, and becomes itself truly beautiful, and thereby rest in the conscious thought of your living union with Christ."

The eleven points discussed above have one purpose: To help us achieve *union without ceasing*. Webster defines union as "an act of joining together, or a state of being united." What actually takes place says St. Teresa of Avila is that "your soul becomes one with God." St. Paul defined union in similar word: "whoever is joined to the Lord becomes one spirit with Him" (1 *Cor* 6:17). The great Indian (Hindu) philosopher Radhakrishnan elaborates further, "The oldest wisdom in the world tells us that we can consciously unite with the divine while in this body, for this is man really born. If he misses his destiny Nature is not in a hurry; she will catch him someday and compel him to fulfill her secret purpose.

We know that our Father is within. He is also without. Just like all the TV and radio programs. To hear or see them we need a tuner. *That tuner to our Father is* Purity (in thought, word and deed), *stillness and love*.

Incidentally, if you are not perfectly aligned on your radio or TV dial you will also be getting noise. Your program will be disturbed. The same is true here. *Your mind has to be emptied of sensations, images, and thoughts.* You have to forget yourself. You have to concentrate on love of God, the Light within your soul, all universe and beyond. *BE STILL* and *LOVE HIM* with all your heart, *BE STILL* and *LOVE HIM* with all your soul, *BE STILL* and *LOVE HIM* with all your power, *BE STILL* and *LOVE HIM* with all your mind (lose yourself in the Beloved) and nothing else.

In this loving embrace and bliss your spirit will be absorbed into Eternal Love. All will become One. Like one light merged in the ocean of Light. You will transcend the uttermost bounds of anticipation or desire. You will have reached a fountain of Holy Joy and Peace so overpowering that it transcends all other joys and passes all understanding. You will have returned to your Father's heart. Similarly you may also concentrate on His Will. Let the Father's will permeate all of you. Let Him make you complete. Let Him exhilarate you. Let Him make you One. In this splendor of joy you will notice that you as such have disappeared. Only His Will, His Love, His Light, has remained.

Initially the state of rapturous union could be momentary, with exhilarating joy and exultation—later on of longer durations (lasting for hours) and extending even into sleep. And eventually you could establish a permanent conscious (living) union with God. The impact of

each experience is most overpowering. It "penetrates to
the very marrow of your bones," testifies Saint Teresa.
"Your senses could be fused into one ineffable act of
perception. Differences between time, space, and motion
will cease to exist. You will understand the profound
truth that there is only God, the I Am Who Am" (Ex
3:14), that "The Father and I are one" (John 10:30),
that "I am in the Father and the Father is in me" (John
14:11), that "the life I live now is not my own; Christ
is living in me" (*Gal* 2:20), that "My Me is God, nor do
I recognize any other Me except my God Himself"
(Saint Catherine of Genoa), that "whoever has seen me
has seen the Father" (John 14:9).

You might find yourself in the center of stillness
and living glow so pronounced that the distinction between you and your surroundings will disappear. You
will see that you and the rest of the surroundings are
one and the same light and stillness, one and the same
Joy of shimmering Conscious Glory and Love. You will
be moving, sitting, and working in it. It is a fantastic
and indescribable splendor of delightful stillness and
peace. The mind thinks—but for some reason all of you
ceases to exist as a separate entity but becomes a part
of one infinite Light and Love. You might dive into an
ocean of knowledge (truth, basic concepts of science,
work of art, inventions) where all that was obscured is
now explained, where all problems are solved, and
all that is or will be knowable is known. All knowledge of above all reason and beyond all thought is
nearer to you than you are to yourself. You have tuned
in to your Father's Heart. "This is the way," said the
voice of God to Saint Catherine of Siena, "If you will
arrive at a perfect knowledge and enjoyment of Me,
the Eternal Truth, you should never go outside the
knowledge of yourself; and by humbling yourself in the

valley of humility you will know Me and yourself, from which knowledge you will draw all that is necessary."

Saint Teresa of Avila, who drank His wine of union, similarly relates: "There will suddenly come to it (soul) a suspension in which the Lord communicates most secret things, which it seems to see within God Himself. . . . The brilliance of this vision is like that of infused light or of a sun covered with some material of the transparency of a diamond. . . . For as long as such a soul is in this state, it can neither see nor hear nor understand: the period is always short and seems to the soul even shorter than it really is. God implants Himself in the interior of that soul in such a way that, when it returns to itself, it cannot possibly doubt that God has been in it and it has been in God; so firmly does this truth remain within it that, although for years God may never grant it that favor again, it can neither forget it nor doubt that it has received it."

St. Catherine of Genoa, who was one of the most penetrating gazers into the secrets of Eternal Light, states: "When the loving kindness of God calls a soul from the world, He finds it full of vices and sins; and first He gives it an instinct for virtue, and then urges it to perfection, and then by infused grace leads it to true self-naughting, and at last to true transformation. And this noteworthy order serves God to lead the soul along the Way; but when the soul is naughted and transformed, then of herself she neither works nor speaks nor wills, nor feels nor hears nor understands, neither has she of herself the feeling of outward or inward, where she may move. And in all things it is God who rules and guides her, without the mediation of any creature. And the state of this soul is then a feeling of such utter peace and tranquility that it seems to her that her heart, and her bodily being, and all both within and without is immersed in an ocean of utmost peace; from when she shall never come forth for anything that can befall her in this life. And she stays immovable, imperturbable, impassable. So much so, that it seems to her in her human and her spiritual nature, both within and without, she can feel no other thing than sweetest peace. And she is so full of peace that though she press her flesh, her nerves, her bones, no other thing comes forth from them than peace."

Having immersed yourself in Perfect Love for a new life and a new purpose, you can't stop here. You have to go on. You have to bring forth your fruits in good deeds. You have to serve others. You have to *treat every person as you would treat Jesus* (see him in every heart and every face. For he said it himself and we shall hear it again in a day of judgment: "I assure you, as often as you did it for one of my least brothers, you did it for me" (*Matt* 25:40). Say nothing, do nothing, think nothing that is not love directed. If what you do, be it in thought, word or deed does not create love, don't do it. Remember, you are not just rendering it to a mortal man but unto God who is within that man.

A note of caution: As you are journeying onward and upward to God (growing in goodness and love), you may come upon many "wine cellars," "fireworks," and "beautiful scenery" full of surprises. As the Bible shows (1 Cor 12:9, 10; 2 Cor 12:1), these by-products could exhibit themselves in many forms:

1. You may speak or interpret tongues.
2. You may experience "visions and revelations," "prophecy," and have the "power to distinguish one spirit from another."
3. You may acquire a new kind of perception where the whole cosmic panorama may appear magnified and full of light and grandeur.

4. Your body sweat may emanate perfumelike fragrance.
5. You may acquire the "healing" touch.
6. You may exhibit bilocation (go to distant places with your body instantaneously—(*John* 20:26–29; Acts 8:39–40). This is possible because as you concentrate on God, His forces dematerialize the body. It becomes less solid and more flexible (your body frequencies increase) and therefore can be more easily acted on by your thought. For additional reading, read about people who had this quality: Saint Ignatius, Saint Clement, Saint Francis of Assisi, Saint Anthony of Padua, Saint Francis Xavier, Joseph Cupertino, Saint Martin de Porres, Saint Alphonsus Liguori, Padre Pio.

These and similar diversions may so overpower you that you will become arrested at this level of growth. True, the dramatic phenomenon is fascinating, but it should *never* become for you the circumference of your horizon. Similarly it is highly dangerous to one's soul and health to seek gifts of this nature for their own sake or for personal enhancement. Let the scenery be there (use it in a constructive way), *but keep in mind your destination is the living union with your Heavenly Father*, and nothing less. And at the union you have to arrive not by expending consciousness with drugs, chemicals and hallucinogens, but through the way of Jesus. With drugs and chemicals you are not improving yourself, you are drowning yourself. You are letting yourself be possessed by saboteur and insidious spirit entities, with results that are far worse after the trip than before the trip. Listen to what the Son of Man had to say about this: "I tell you the truth: whoever does not enter the sheepfold by the door, but climbs in some other way, is a thief and a marauder. To get there," said He,

"I am the door. Whoever enters through me will be safe. He will go in and out and find pasture" (*John* 10:9). Similarly Jesus reproached the Pharisees, most of whom were ignorant of union, yet deliberately obstructed the helpless masses: "Woe to you lawyers! You have taken away the key of knowledge. You yourselves have not gained access, yet you have stopped those who wish to enter!" (*Luke* 11:52) The key to union you will find only through crucifying your self-love and self-will. Jesus demonstrated this with his death on the cross and demanded that we do the same: "Whoever wishes to be my follower must *deny his very self,* take up his cross each day" (not the cross of suffering, but the self-crucifixion), and "and follow in my steps" (*Luke* 9:23).

True, the lower self doesn't want to die, it wants to live, it wants Father to take that cup away, but your conscious self knows that "for he who wishes to save his life must lose it," he must destroy the lower self so that it will not be the deciding guide, but the Higher Will, the Father's Will, will be the way.

You have to consciously live in His Presence, a life of Jesus Christ (make iron determination to be pure within), a life of "be perfect just as your Father in heaven is perfect" (perfect in love), continuously a life of *LOVE IN ACTION* (love everything because it needs love like you; your Father has programmed "the branches" that way, so "that all may be one . . . as we are one") . . . one day at a time . . . now. The reward of this type of life is union without ceasing, where Eternal Love and you will be One, where heaven and all glory will exist here and now, where the state of joy, splendor, bliss, tranquillity, and overpowering peace will be with you every moment, where with tears in your eyes, you the Prodigal Son will be embraced by your Beloved Father on your welcome home, where with a might of Christ you will proclaim: "Eli, Eli, lmana shabachthani! . . . . My God, My God, this was my destiny. I was born for this." Then you will know this chapter "is finished." Now a new chapter of Resurrection, Light and Unity is upon you.

I LOVE YOU!

BASIC SOURCES

The New American Bible, Copyright © 1970 by Confraternity of Christian Doctrine, The Catholic Press, Washington D.C.
Good News for Modern Man.
Today's Version of The New Testament, Copyright © American Bible Society, 1966, 1971.

THE LORD'S PRAYER

Our Father, which art in heaven, Hallowed be thy name. Thy kingdom come. Thy will be done, in earth as it is in heaven. Give us this day our daily bread. And forgive us our trespasses, as we forgive them that trespass against us. And lead us not into temptation; but deliver us from evil: For thine is the kingdom, the power, and the glory, for ever and ever.

Amen.

Emmet Fox

The Lord's Prayer is a distillation of all Christian theology. Here Dr. Emmet Fox examines this concise vehicle for progress through the whole of spiritual life.

Dr. Fox was one of the outstanding spiritual teachers of our times. While he lived he addressed some of the largest audiences ever gathered to hear one man's thoughts on the religious meaning of life. He published extensively, and some of his best known works are *The Sermon on the Mount, The Ten Commandments, Alter Your Life, Power Through Constructive Thinking, Make Your Life Worth-while* and *Find and Use Your Inner Power.*

The Lord's Prayer is the most important of all the Christian documents. It was carefully constructed by

Jesus with certain very clear ends in view. That is why, of all his teachings, it is by far the best known and the most often quoted. It is, indeed, the one common denominator of all the Christian churches. Every one of them, without exception, uses the Lord's Prayer; it is perhaps the only ground upon which they all meet. Every Christian child is taught the Lord's Prayer, and any Christian who prays at all says it almost every day. Its actual use probably exceeds that of all other prayers put together. Undoubtedly, everyone who is seeking to follow along the Way that Jesus led, should make a point of using the Lord's Prayer, and using it intelligently, every day.

In order to do this, we should understand that the Prayer is a carefully constructed organic whole. Many people rattle through it like parrots, forgetful of the warning that Jesus gave us against vain repetitions, and, of course, no one derives any profit from that sort of thing.

The Great Prayer is a compact formula for the development of the soul. It is designed with the utmost care for that specific purpose; so that those who use it regularly, with understanding, will experience a real change of soul. The only progress is this change, which is what the Bible calls being born again. It is the change of soul that matters. The mere acquisition of fresh knowledge received intellectually makes no change in the soul. The Lord's Prayer is especially designed to bring this change about, and when it is regularly used it invariably does so.

The more one analyzes the Lord's Prayer, the more wonderful is its construction seen to be. It meets everyone's need just at his own level. It not only provides a rapid spiritual development for those who are sufficiently advanced to be ready, but in its superficial meaning it supplies the more simple-minded and even the more materially-minded people with just what they need at the moment, if they use the Prayer sincerely.

This greatest of all prayers was designed with still another purpose in view, quite as important as either of the others. Jesus foresaw that, as the centuries went by, his simple, primitive teaching would gradually become overlaid by all sorts of external things which really have nothing whatever to do with it. He foresaw that men who had never known him, relying, quite sincerely, no doubt, upon their own limited intellects, would build up theologies and doctrinal systems, obscuring the direct simplicity of the spiritual message, and actually erecting a wall between God and man. He designed his Prayer in such a way that it would pass safely through those ages without being tampered with. He arranged it with consummate skill, so that it could not be twisted or distorted, or adapted to any man-made system; so that, in fact, it would carry the whole Christ Message within it, and yet not have anything on the surface to attract the attention of the restless, managing type of person. So it has turned out that, through all the changes and chances of Christian history, this Prayer has come through to us uncorrupted and unspoiled.

The first thing that we notice is that the Prayer naturally falls into seven clauses. This is very characteristic of the Oriental tradition. Seven symbolizes individual completeness, the perfection of the individual soul, just as the number twelve in the same convention stands for corporate completeness. In practical use, we often find an eighth clause added—"Thine is the kingdom, the power, and the glory"—but this, though in itself an excellent affirmation, is not really a part of the Prayer. The seven clauses are put together with the utmost care, in perfect order and sequence, and they contain everything that is necessary for the nourishment of the soul. Let us consider the first clause:

Our Father

This simple statement in itself constitutes a definite and complete system of theology. It fixes clearly and distinctly the nature and character of God. It sums up the Truth of Being. It tells all that man needs to know about God, and about himself, and about his neighbor. Anything that is added to this can only be by way of commentary, and is more likely than not to complicate and obscure the true meaning of the text. Oliver Wendell Holmes said: "My religion is summed up in the first two words of the Lord's Prayer," and most of us will find ourselves in full agreement with him.

Notice the simple, clear-cut, definite statement— "Our Father." In this clause Jesus lays down once and for all that the relationship between God and man is that of father and child. This cuts out any possibility that the Deity could be the relentless and cruel tyrant that is often pictured by theology. Jesus says definitely that the relationship is that of parent and child; not an Oriental despot dealing with grovelling slaves, but parent and child. Now we all know perfectly well that men and women, however short they may fall in other respects, nearly always do the best they can for their children. Unfortunately, cruel and wicked parents are to be found, but they are so exceptional as to make a paragraph for the newspapers. The vast majority of men and women are at their best in dealing with their children. Speaking of the same truth elsewhere, Jesus said: "If you, who are so full of evil, nevertheless do your best for your children, how much more will God, who is al-

together good, do for you"; and so he begins his Prayer
by establishing the character of God as that of the perfect Father dealing with His children.

Note that this clause which fixes the nature of God,
at the same time fixes the nature of man, because if man
is the offspring of God, he must partake of the nature of
God, since the nature of the offspring is invariably similar to that of the parent. It is a cosmic law that like be-
gets like. It is not possible that a rosebush should produce lilies, or that a cow should give birth to a colt. The
offspring is and must be of the same nature as the
parent; and so, since God is Divine Spirit, man must essentially be Divine Spirit too, whatever appearances
may say to the contrary.

Let us pause here for a moment and try to realize
what a tremendous step forward we have taken in ap-
preciating the teaching of Jesus on this point. Do you
not see that at a single blow it swept away ninety-nine
per cent of all the old theology, with its avenging God,
its chosen and favored individuals, its eternal hell-fire,
and all the other horrible paraphernalia of man's dis-
eased and terrified imagination. God exists—and the
Eternal, All-Powerful, All-Present God is the loving
Father of mankind.

If you would meditate upon this fact until you had
some degree of understanding of what it really means,
most of your difficulties and physical ailments would
disappear, for they are rooted and grounded in fear.
The underlying cause of all trouble is fear. If only you
could realize to some extent that Omnipotent Wisdom is
your living, loving Father, most of your fears would go.
If you could realize it completely, every negative thing
in your life would vanish away, and you would demon-
strate perfection in every phase. Now you see the object
that Jesus had in mind when he placed this clause first.

Next we see that the Prayer says not "My Father," but "Our Father," and this indicates, beyond the possibility of mistake, the truth of the brotherhood of man. It forces upon our attention at the very beginning the fact that all men are indeed brethren, the children of one Father; and that "there is neither Jew nor Greek, there is neither bond nor free, there is neither chosen nor unchosen," because all men are brethren. Here Jesus, in making his second point, ends all the tiresome nonsense about a "chosen race," about the spiritual superiority of any one group of human beings over any other group. He cuts away the illusion that the members of any nation, or race, or territory, or group, or class, or color, are, in the sight of God, superior to any other group. A belief in the superiority of one's own particular group, or "herd," as the psychologists call it, is an illusion to which mankind is very prone, but in the teaching of Jesus it has no place. He teaches that the thing that places a man is the spiritual condition of his own individual soul, and that as long as he is upon the spiritual path it makes no difference whatever to what group he belongs or does not belong.

The final point is the implied command that we are to pray not only for ourselves but for all mankind. Every student of Truth should hold the thought of the Truth of Being for the whole human race for at least a moment each day, since none of us lives to himself nor dies to himself; for indeed we are all truly—and in a much more literal sense than people are aware—limbs of one Body.

Now we begin to see how very much more than appears on the surface is contained in those simple words "Our Father." Simple—one might almost say innocent—as they look, Jesus has concealed within them a spiritual explosive that will ultimately destroy every

man-made system that holds the human race in bondage.

Which art in heaven

Having clearly established the Fatherhood of God
and the brotherhood of man, Jesus next goes on to enlarge upon the nature of God, and to describe the fundamental facts of existence. Having shown that God
and man are parent and child, he goes on to delineate
the function of each in the grand scheme of things. He
explains that it is the nature of God to be in heaven,
and of man to be on earth, because God is Cause, and
man is manifestation. Cause cannot be expression, and
expression cannot be cause, and we must be careful not
to confuse the two things. Here heaven stands for God
or Cause, because in religious phraseology heaven is the
term for the Presence of God. In metaphysics it is called
the Absolute, because it is the realm of Pure Uncondi-
tioned Being, of archetypal ideas. The word "earth"
means manifestation, and man's function is to manifest
or express God, or Cause. In other words, God is the
Infinite and Perfect Cause of all things; but Cause has
to be expressed, and God expresses Himself by means
of man. Man's destiny is to express God in all sorts of
glorious and wonderful ways. Some of this expression
we see as his surroundings; first his physical body,
which is really only the most intimate part of his em-
bodiment; then his home; his work; his recreation; in
short, his whole expression. To express means to press
outwards, or bring into sight that which already exists
implicitly. Every feature of your life is really a manifestation or expression of something in your soul.

Some of these points may seem at first to be a little

abstract; but since it is misunderstandings about the relationship of God and man that lead to all our difficulties, it is worth any amount of trouble to understand correctly that relationship. Trying to have manifestation without Cause is atheism and materialism, and we know where they lead. Trying to have Cause without manifestation leads man to suppose himself to be a personal God, and this commonly ends in megalomania and a kind of paralysis of expression.

The important thing to realize is that God is in heaven and man on earth, and that each has his own role in the scheme of things. Although they are One, they are not one-and-the-same. Jesus establishes this point carefully when he says, "Our Father which art in heaven."

Hallowed be thy name

In the Bible, as elsewhere, the "name" of anything means the essential nature or character of that thing, and so, when we are told what the name of God is, we are told what His nature is, and His name or nature, Jesus says, is "hallowed." Now what does the word "hallowed" mean? Well, if you trace the derivation back into Old English, you will discover a most extraordinarily interesting and significant fact. The word "hallowed" has the same meaning as "holy," "whole," "wholesome," and "heal," or "healed"; so we see that the nature of God is not merely worthy of our veneration, but is complete and perfect—altogether good. Some very remarkable consequences follow from this. We have agreed that an effect must be similar in its nature to its cause, and so, because the nature of God is hallowed, everything that follows from that Cause must be hallowed or perfect, too. Just as a rosebush cannot produce lilies, so God cannot cause or send anything but perfect good. As the Bible says, "the same fountain cannot send forth both sweet and bitter water." From this it follows that God cannot, as people sometimes think, send sickness or trouble or accidents—much less death—for these things are unlike His nature. "Hallowed be thy name" means "Thy nature is altogether good, and Thou art the author only of perfect good." Of purer eyes than to behold evil, and canst not look on iniquity.

If you think that God has sent any of your difficulties to you, for no matter how good a reason, you are giving power to your troubles, and this makes it very difficult to get rid of them.

Thy kingdom come.
Thy will be done
in earth as it is in heaven

Man, being manifestation or expression of God, has a limitless destiny before him. His work is to express, in concrete, definite form, the abstract ideas with which God furnishes him, and in order to do this, he must have creative power. If he did not have creative power, he would be merely a machine through which God worked—an automaton. But man is not an automaton; he is an individualized consciousness. God individualizes Himself in an infinite number of distinct focal points of consciousness, each one quite different; and therefore each one is a distinct way of knowing the universe, each a distinct experience. Notice carefully that the word "individual" means undivided. The consciousness of each one is distinct from God and from all others, and yet none are separated. How can this be? How can two things be one, and yet not one and the same? The answer is that in matter, which is finite, they cannot; but in Spirit, which is infinite, they can. With our present limited, three-dimensional consciousness, we cannot see this; but intuitively we can understand it through prayer. If God did not individualize Himself, there would be only one experience; as it is, there are as many universes as there are individuals to form them through thinking.

"Thy kingdom come" means that it is our duty to be ever occupied in helping to establish the Kingdom of God on earth. That is to say, our work is to bring more and more of God's ideas into concrete manifestation upon this plane. That is what we are here for. The old saying, "God has a plan for every man, and he has one for you," is quite correct. God has glorious and wonderful plans for every one of us; He has planned a splendid career, full of interest, life, and joy, for each, and if our lives are dull, or restricted, or squalid, that is not His fault, but ours.

If only you will find out the thing God intends you to do, and will do it, you will find that all doors will open to you; all obstacles in your path will melt away; you will be acclaimed a brilliant success; you will be most liberally rewarded from the monetary point of view; and you will be gloriously happy.

There is a true place in life for each one of us, upon the attainment of which we shall be completely happy, and perfectly secure. On the other hand, until we do find our true place we never shall be either happy or secure, no matter what other things we may have. Our true place is the one place where we can bring the Kingdom of God into manifestation, and truly say, "Thy kingdom cometh."

We have seen that man too often chooses to use his

free will in a negative way. He allows himself to think wrongly, selfishly, and this wrong thinking brings upon him all his troubles. Instead of understanding that it is his essential nature to express God, to be ever about his Father's business, he tries to set up upon his own account. All our troubles arise from just this folly. We abuse our free will, trying to work apart from God; and the very natural result is all the sickness, poverty, sin, trouble, and death that we find on the physical plane. We must never for a moment try to live for ourselves, or make plans or arrangements without reference to God, or suppose that we can be either happy or successful if we are seeking any other end than to do His Will. Whatever our desire may be, whether it be something concerning our daily work, or our duty at home, our relations with our fellow man, or private plans for the employment of our own time, if we seek to serve self instead of God, we are ordering trouble, disappointment, and unhappiness, notwithstanding what the evidence to the contrary may seem to be. Whereas, if we choose what, through prayer, we know to be His Will, then we are insuring for ourselves ultimate success, freedom, and joy, however much self-sacrifice and self-discipline it may involve at the moment.

Our business is to bring our whole nature as fast as we can into conformity with the Will of God, by constant prayer and unceasing, though unanxious, watching. "Our wills are ours to make them Thine."

"In His Will is our peace," said Dante, and the Divine Comedy is really a study in fundamental states of consciousness, the Inferno representing the state of the soul that is endeavoring to live without God, the Paradiso representing the state of the soul that has achieved its conscious unity with the Divine Will, and the Purgatorio the condition of the soul that is struggling

to pass from the one state to the other. It was this sublime conflict of the soul which wrung from the heart of
the great Augustine the cry "Thou hast made us for
Thyself, and our hearts are restless until they repose in
Thee."

Give us this day
our daily bread

Because we are the children of a loving Father, we
are entitled to expect that God will provide us fully with
everything we need. Children naturally and spontaneously look to their human parents to supply all their
wants, and in the same way we should look to God to
supply ours. If we do so, in faith and understanding, we
shall never look in vain.

It is the Will of God that we should all lead healthy,
happy lives, full of joyous experience; that we should
develop freely and steadily, day by day and week by
week, as our pathways unfold more and more unto the
perfect day. To this end we require such things as food,
clothing, shelter, means of travel, books, and so on;
above all, we require freedom; and in the Prayer all
these things are included under the heading of bread.
Bread, that is to say, means not merely food in general,
but all things that man requires for a healthy, happy,
free, and harmonious life. But in order to obtain these
things, we have to claim them, not necessarily in detail,
but we have to claim them, and we have to recognize
God and God alone as the Source and fountainhead of
all our good. Lack of any kind is always traceable to the
fact that we have been seeking our supply from some
secondary source, instead of from God, Himself, the
Author and Giver of life.

People think of their supply as coming from certain investments, or from a business, or from an employer, perhaps; whereas these are merely the channels through which it comes, God being the Source. The number of possible channels is infinite, the Source is One. The particular channel through which you are getting your supply is quite likely to change, because change is the Cosmic Law for manifestation. Stagnation is really death; but as long as you realize that the Source of your supply is the one unchangeable Spirit, all is well. The fading out of one channel will be but the signal for the opening of another. If, on the other hand, like most people, you regard the particular channel as being the source, then when that channel fails, as it is very likely to do, you are left stranded, because you believe that the source has dried up—and for practical purposes, on the physical plane, things are as we believe them to be.

A man, for instance, thinks of his employment as the source of his income, and for some reason he loses it. His employer goes out of business, or cuts down the staff, or they have a falling out. Now, because he believes that his position is the source of his income, the loss of the position naturally means the loss of the income, and so he has to start looking about for another job, and perhaps has to look a long time, meanwhile finding himself without apparent supply. If such a man had realized, through regular daily Treatment, that God was his supply, and his job only the particular channel through which it came, then upon the closing of that channel, he would have found another, and probably a better one, opening immediately. If his belief had been in God as his supply, then since God cannot change or fail, or fade out, his supply would have come from somewhere, and would have formed its own channel in whatever was the easiest way.

In precisely the same way the proprietor of a business may find himself obliged to close down for some cause outside of his control; or one whose income is dependent upon stocks or bonds may suddenly find that source dried up, owing to unexpected happenings on the stock market, or to some catastrophe to a factory or a mine. If he regards the business or the investment as his source of supply, he will believe his source to have collapsed, and will in consequence be left stranded; whereas, if his reliance is upon God, he will be comparatively indifferent to the channel and so that channel will be easily supplanted by a new one. In short, we have to train ourselves to look to God, Cause, for all that we need, and then the channel, which is entirely a secondary matter, will take care of itself.

In its inner and most important meaning, our daily bread signifies the realization of the Presence of God—an actual sense that God exists not merely in a nominal way, but as the great reality; the sense that He is present with us; and the feeling that because He is God, all good, all powerful, all wise, and all loving, we have nothing to fear; that we can rely upon Him to take every care of us; that He will supply all that we need to have; teach us all that we need to know; and guide our steps so that we shall not make mistakes. This is Emanuel, or God with us; and remember that it absolutely means some degree of actual realization, that is to say, some experience in consciousness, and not just a theoretical recognition of the fact; not simply talking about God, however beautifully one may talk, or thinking about Him; but some degree of actual experience. We must begin by thinking about God, but this should lead to the realization which is the daily bread or manna. That is the gist of the whole matter. Realization, which is experience, is the thing that counts. It is realization which marks the progress of the soul. It is realization which guarantees the demonstration. It is realization, as distinct from mere theorizing and fine words, which is the substance of things hoped for, the evidence of things not seen. This is the Bread of Life, the hidden manna, and when one has that, he has all things in deed and in truth. Jesus several times refers to this experience as bread because it is the nourishment of the soul, just as physical food is the nourishment of the physical body. Supplied with this food, the soul grows and waxes strong, gradually developing to adult stature. Without it, she, being deprived of the essential nourishment, is naturally stunted and crippled.

The common mistake, of course, is to suppose that a formal recognition of God is sufficient, or that talking about Divine things, perhaps talking very poetically, is the same as possessing them; but this is exactly on a par with supposing that looking at a tray of food, or discussing the chemical composition of sundry foodstuffs, is the same thing as actually eating a meal. It is this mistake which is responsible for the fact that people sometimes pray for a thing for years without any tangible result. If prayer is a force at all, it cannot be possible to pray without something happening.

A realization cannot be obtained to order; it must come spontaneously as the result of regular daily prayer. To seek realization by will power is the surest way to miss it. Pray regularly and quietly—remember that in all mental work, effort or strain defeats itself— then presently, perhaps when you least expect it, like a thief in the night, the realization will come. Meanwhile it is well to know that all sorts of practical difficulties can be overcome by sincere prayer, without any realization at all. Good workers have said that they have had some of their best demonstrations without any realization worth speaking about; but while it is, of course, a wonderful boon to surmount such particular difficulties, we do not achieve the sense of security and well-being to which we are entitled until we have experienced realization.

Another reason why the food or bread symbol for the experience of the Presence of God is such a telling one, is that the act of eating food is essentially a thing that must be done for oneself. No one can assimilate food for another. One may hire servants to do all sorts of other things for him; but there is one thing that one must positively do for himself, and that is to eat his own food. In the same way, the realization of the Presence of God is a thing that no one else can have for us. We can and should help one another in the overcoming of specific difficulties—"Bear ye one another's burdens"— but the realization (or making real) of the Presence of God, the "substance" and "evidence," can, in the nature of things, be had only at first hand.

In speaking of the "bread of life, Emanuel," Jesus calls it our daily bread. The reason for this is very fundamental—our contact with God must be a living one. It is our momentary attitude to God which governs our being. "Behold now is the accepted time; behold now is the day of salvation." The most futile thing in the world is to seek to live upon a past realization. The thing that means spiritual life to you is your realization of God here and now.

Today's realization, no matter how feeble and poor it may seem, has a million times more power to help you than the most vivid realization of yesterday. Be thankful for yesterday's experience, knowing that it is with you forever in the change of consciousness which it brought about, but do not lean upon it for a single moment for the need of today. Divine Spirit is and changes not with the ebb and flow of human apprehension. The manna in the desert is the Old Testament prototype of this. The people wandering in the wilderness were told that they would be supplied with manna from heaven every day, each one always receiving abundant for his needs, but they were on no account to try to save it up for the morrow. They were on no account to endeavor to live upon yesterday's food, and when, notwithstanding the rule, some of them did try to do so, the result was pestilence or death.

So it is with us. When we seek to live upon yesterday's realization, we are actually seeking to live in the past, and to live in the past is death. The art of life is to live in the present moment, and to make that moment as perfect as we can by the realization that we are the instruments and expression of God Himself. The best way to prepare for tomorrow is to make today all that it should be.

Forgive us our trespasses, as we forgive them that trespass against us

This clause is the turning point of the Prayer. It is the strategic key to the whole Treatment. Let us notice here that Jesus has so arranged this marvelous Prayer that it covers the entire ground of the unfoldment of our souls completely, and in the most concise and telling way. It omits nothing that is essential for our salvation, and yet, so compact is it that there is not a thought or a word too much. Every idea fits into its place with perfect harmony and in perfect sequence. Anything more would be redundance, anything less would be incompleteness, and at this point it takes up the critical factor of forgiveness.

Having told us what God is, what man is, how the universe works, how we are to do our own work—the salvation of humanity and of our own souls—he then explains what our true nourishment or supply is, and the way in which we can obtain it; and now he comes to the forgiveness of sins.

The forgiveness of sins is the central problem of life. Sin is a sense of separation from God, and is the major tragedy of human experience. It is, of course, rooted in selfishness. It is essentially an attempt to gain some supposed good to which we are not entitled in justice. It is a sense of isolated, self-regarding, personal existence, whereas the Truth of Being is that all is One. Our true selves are at one with God, undivided from Him, expressing His ideas, witnessing to His nature—the dynamic Thinking of that Mind. Because we are all one with the great Whole of which we are spiritually a part, it follows that we are one with all men. Just because in Him we live and move and have our being, we are, in the absolute sense, all essentially one.

Evil, sin, the fall of man, in fact, is essentially the attempt to negate this Truth in our thoughts. We try to live apart from God. We try to do without Him. We act as though we had life of our own; as separate minds; as though we could have plans and purposes and interests separate from His. All this, if it were true, would mean that existence is not one and harmonious, but a chaos of competition and strife. It would mean that we are quite separate from our fellow man and could injure him, rob him, hurt him, or even destroy him, without any damage to ourselves, and, in fact, that the more we took from other people the more we should have for ourselves. It would mean that the more we considered our own interests, and the more indifferent we were to the welfare of others, the better off we should be. Of course it would then follow naturally that it would pay others to treat us in the same way, and that accordingly we might expect many of them to do so. Now if this were true, it would mean that the whole universe is only a jungle, and that sooner or later it must destroy itself by its own inherent weakness and anarchy. But, of course, it is not true, and therein lies the joy of life.

Undoubtedly, many people do act as though they believe it to be true, and a great many more, who would be dreadfully shocked if brought face to face with that proposition in cold blood, have, nevertheless, a vague feeling that such must be very much the way things are, even though they, themselves, are personally above consciously acting in accordance with such a notion. Now this is the real basis of sin, of resentment, of condemnation, of jealousy, of remorse, and all the evil brood that walk that path.

This belief in independent and separate existence is the arch sin, and now, before we can progress any further, we have to take the knife to this evil thing and cut it out once and for all. Jesus knew this, and with this definite end in view he inserted at this critical point a carefully prepared statement that would compass our end and his, without the shadow of a possibility of miscarrying. He inserted what is nothing less than a trip clause. He drafted a declaration which would force us, without any conceivable possibility of escape, evasion, mental reservation, or subterfuge of any kind, to execute the great sacrament of forgiveness in all its fullness and far-reaching power.

As we repeat the Great Prayer intelligently, considering and meaning what we say, we are suddenly, so to speak, caught up off our feet and grasped as though in a vise, so that we must face this problem—and there is no escape. We must positively and definitely extend forgiveness to everyone to whom it is possible that we can owe forgiveness, namely, to anyone who we think can have injured us in any way. Jesus leaves no room for any possible glossing of this fundamental thing. He has constructed his Prayer with more skill than ever yet lawyer displayed in the casting of a deed. He has so contrived it that once our attention has been drawn to this matter, we are inevitably obliged either to forgive our enemies in sincerity and truth, or never again to repeat that prayer. It is safe to say that no one who reads this essay with understanding will ever again be able to use the Lord's Prayer unless and until he has forgiven. Should you now attempt to repeat it without forgiving, it can safely be predicted that you will not be able to finish it. This great central clause will stick in your throat.

Notice that Jesus does not say, "Forgive me my trespasses and I will try to forgive others," or "I will see if it can be done," or "I will forgive generally, with certain exceptions." He obliges us to declare that we have actually forgiven, and forgiven all, and he makes our claim to our own forgiveness to depend upon that. Who is there who has grace enough to say his prayers at all, who does not long for the forgiveness or cancellation of his own mistakes and faults. Who would be so insane as to endeavor to seek the Kingdom of God without desiring to be relieved of his own sense of guilt. No one, we may believe. And so we see that we are trapped in the inescapable position that we cannot demand our own release before we have released our brother.

The forgiveness of others is the vestibule of Heaven, and Jesus knew it, and has led us to the door. You must forgive everyone who has ever hurt you if you want to be forgiven yourself; that is the long and the short of it.

You have to get rid of all resentment and condemnation of others, and, not least, of self-condemnation and remorse. You have to forgive others, and having discontinued your own mistakes, you have to accept the forgiveness of God for them too, or you cannot make any progress. You have to forgive yourself, but you cannot forgive yourself sincerely until you have forgiven others first. Having forgiven others, you must be prepared to forgive yourself too, for to refuse to forgive oneself is only spiritual pride. "And by that sin fell the angels." We cannot make this point too clear to ourselves; we have got to forgive. There are few people in the world who have not at some time or other been hurt, really hurt, by someone else; or been disappointed, or injured, or deceived, or misled. Such things sink into the memory where they usually cause inflamed and festering wounds, and there is only one remedy—they have to be plucked out and thrown away. And the one and only way to do that is by forgiveness.

Of course, nothing in all the world is easier than to forgive people who have not hurt us very much. Nothing is easier than to rise above the thought of a trifling loss. Anybody will be willing to do this, but what the Law of Being requires of us is that we forgive not only these trifles, but the very things that are so hard to forgive that at first it seems impossible to do it at all. The despairing heart cries, "It is too much to ask. That thing meant too much to me. It is impossible. I cannot forgive it." But the Lord's Prayer makes our own forgiveness from God, which means our escape from guilt and limitation, dependent upon just this very thing. There is no escape from this, and so forgiveness there must be, no matter how deeply we may have been injured, or how terribly we have suffered. It must be done.

If your prayers are not being answered, search your

consciousness and see if there is not someone whom you have yet to forgive. Find out if there is not some old thing about which you are very resentful. Search and see if you are not really holding a grudge (it may be camouflaged in some self-righteous way) against some individual, or some body of people, a nation, a race, a social class, some religious movement of which you disapprove perhaps, a political party, or what-not. If you are doing so, then you have an act of forgiveness to perform and when this is done, you will probably make your demonstration. If you cannot forgive at present, you will have to wait for your demonstration until you can, and you will have to postpone finishing your recital of the Lord's Prayer too, or involve yourself in the position that you do not desire the forgiveness of God.

Setting others free means setting yourself free, because resentment is really a form of attachment. It is a Cosmic Truth that it takes two to make a prisoner; the prisoner—and a gaoler. There is no such thing as being a prisoner on one's own account. Every prisoner must have a gaoler, and the gaoler is as much a prisoner as his charge. When you hold resentment against anyone, you are bound to that person by a cosmic link, a real, though mental chain. You are tied by a cosmic tie to the thing that you hate. The one person perhaps in the whole world whom you most dislike is the very one to whom you are attaching yourself by a hook that is stronger than steel. Is this what you wish? Is this the condition in which you desire to go on living? Remember, you belong to the thing with which you are linked in thought, and at some time or other, if that tie endures, the object of your resentment will be drawn again into your life, perhaps to work further havoc. Do you think that you can afford this? Of course, no one can afford such a thing; and so the way is clear. You

must cut all such ties, by a clear and spiritual act of forgiveness. You must loose him and let him go. By forgiveness you set yourself free; you save your soul. And
because the law of love works alike for one and all, you
help to save his soul too, making it just so much easier
for him to become what he ought to be.

But how, in the name of all that is wise and good, is
the magic act of forgiveness to be accomplished, when
we have been so deeply injured that, though we have
long wished with all our hearts that we could forgive,
we have nevertheless found it impossible; when we have
tried and tried to forgive, but have found the task
beyond us.

The technique of forgiveness is simple enough, and
not very difficult to manage when you understand how.
The only thing that is essential is willingness to forgive.
Provided you desire to forgive the offender, the greater
part of the work is already done. People have always
made such a bogey of forgiveness because they have
been under the erroneous impression that to forgive a
person means that you have to compel yourself to like
him. Happily this is by no means the case—we are not
called upon to like anyone whom we do not find ourselves liking spontaneously, and, indeed, it is quite impossible to like people to order. You can no more like
to order than you can hold the winds in your fist, and if
you endeavor to coerce yourself into doing so, you will
finish by disliking or hating the offender more than ever.
People used to think that when someone had hurt them
very much, it was their duty, as good Christians, to
pump up, as it were, a feeling of liking for him; and
since such a thing is utterly impossible, they suffered a
great deal of distress, and ended, necessarily, with fail-
ure, and a resulting sense of sinfulness. We are not obliged to like anyone; but we are under a binding obliga-

tion to love everyone, love, or charity as the Bible calls it, meaning a vivid sense of impersonal good will. This has nothing directly to do with the feelings, though it is always followed, sooner or later, by a wonderful feeling of peace and happiness.

The method of forgiving is this: Get by yourself and become quiet. Repeat any prayer or treatment that appeals to you, or read a chapter of the Bible. Then quietly say, "I fully and freely forgive X (mentioning the name of the offender); I loose him and let him go. I completely forgive the whole business in question. As far as I am concerned, it is finished forever. I cast the burden of resentment upon the Christ within me. He is free now, and I am free too. I wish him well in every phase of his life. That incident is finished. The Christ Truth has set us both free. I thank God." Then get up and go about your business. On no account repeat this act of forgiveness, because you have done it once and for all, and to do it a second time would be tacitly to repudiate your own work. Afterward, whenever the memory of the offender or the offense happens to come into your mind, bless the delinquent briefly and dismiss the thought. Do this, however many times the thought may come back. After a few days it will return less and less often, until you forget it altogether. Then, perhaps after an interval, shorter or longer, the old trouble may come back to memory once more, but you will find that now all bitterness and resentment have disappeared, and you are both free with the perfect freedom of the children of God. Your forgiveness is complete. You will experience a wonderful joy in the realization of the demonstration.

Everybody should practise general forgiveness every day as a matter of course. When you say your daily prayers, issue a general amnesty, forgiving everyone who may have injured you in any way, and on no ac-

count particularize. Simply say: "I freely forgive everyone." Then in the course of the day, should the thought
of grievance or resentment come up, bless the offender
briefly and dismiss the thought.

The result of this policy will be that very soon you
will find yourself cleared of all resentment and condemnation, and the effect upon your happiness, your bodily
health, and your general life will be nothing less than
revolutionary.

Lead us not into temptation
but deliver us from evil

This clause has probably caused more difficulty than
any other part of the Prayer. For many earnest people it
has been a veritable stumbling block. They feel, and
rightly, that God could not lead anyone into temptation
or into evil in any circumstances, and so these words do
not ring true.

For this reason, a number of attempts have been
made to recast the wording. People have felt that Jesus
could not have said what he is represented to have said,
and so they look about for some phrasing which they
think would be more in accordance with the general
tone of his teaching. Heroic efforts have been made to
wrest the Greek original into something different. All
this, however, is unnecessary. The Prayer in the form in
which we have it in English gives a perfectly correct
sense of the true inner meaning. Remember that the
Lord's Prayer covers the whole of the spiritual life.
Condensed though the form is, it is nevertheless a complete manual for the development of the soul, and Jesus
knew only too well the subtle perils and difficulties that
can and do beset the soul when once the preliminary

stages of spiritual unfoldment have been passed. Because those who are yet at a comparatively early stage of development do not experience such difficulties, they are apt to jump to the conclusion that this clause is unnecessary; but such is not the case.

The facts are these—the more you pray, the more time you spend in meditation and spiritual treatment, the more sensitive you become. And if you spend a great deal of time working on your soul in the right way, you will become very sensitive. This is excellent; but like everything in the universe, it works both ways. The more sensitive and spiritual you become, the more powerful and effective are your prayers, you do better healing, and you advance rapidly. But, for the same reason, you also become susceptible to forms of temptation that simply do not beset those at an earlier stage. You will also find that for ordinary faults, even things that many men and women of the world would consider to be trifling, you will be sharply punished, and this is well, because it keeps you up to the mark. The seemingly minor transgressions, the "little foxes that spoil the vines," would fritter away our spiritual power if not promptly dealt with.

No one at this level will be tempted to pick a pocket, or burgle a house; but this does not by any means imply that one will not have difficulties, and because of their subtlety, even greater difficulties to meet.

As we advance, new and powerful temptations await us on the path, ever ready to hurl us down if we are not watchful—temptations to work for self-glory and self-aggrandizement instead of for God; for personal honors and distinctions, even for material gain; temptations to allow personal preferences to hold sway in our counsels when it is a sacred duty to deal with all men in perfect impartiality. Above and beyond all other sins the deadly sin of spiritual pride, truly "the last infirmity of noble mind," lurks on this road. Many fine souls who have triumphantly surmounted all other testings have lapsed into a condition of superiority and self-righteousness that has fallen like a curtain of steel between them and God. Great knowledge brings great responsibility. Great responsibility betrayed brings terrible punishment in its train. Noblesse oblige is preeminently true in spiritual things. One's knowledge of the Truth, however little it may be, is a sacred trust for humanity that must not be violated. While we should never make the mistake of casting our pearls before swine, nor urge the Truth in quarters where it is not welcome, yet we must do all that we wisely can to spread the true knowledge of God among mankind, that not one of "these little ones" may go hungry through our selfishness or our neglect. "Feed my lambs, feed my sheep."

The old occult writers were so vividly sensible of these dangers that, with their instinct for dramatization, they spoke of the soul as being challenged by various tests as it traversed the upward road. It was as though the traveller were halted at various gates or turnpike bars, and tested by some ordeal to determine whether he were ready to advance any further. If he succeeded in passing the test, they said, he was allowed to continue upon his way with the blessing of the challenger. If, however, he failed to survive the ordeal, he was forbidden to proceed.

Now, some less experienced souls, eager for rapid advancement, have rashly desired to be subjected immediately to all kinds of tests, and have even looked about, seeking for difficulties to overcome; as though one's own personality did not already present quite enough material for any one man or woman to deal with. Forgetting the lesson of our Lord's own ordeal in the wilderness, forgetting the injunction "Thou shalt not tempt the Lord thy God," they have virtually done this very thing, with sad results. And so Jesus has inserted this clause, in which we pray that we may not have to meet anything that is too much for us at the present level of our understanding. And, if we are wise, and work daily, as we should, for wisdom, understanding, purity, and the guidance of the Holy Spirit, we never shall find ourselves in any difficulty for which we have not the understanding necessary to clear ourselves. Nothing shall by any means hurt you. Behold I am with you alway.

Thine is the kingdom and the power and the glory for ever and ever

This is a wonderful gnomic saying summing up the essential truth of the Omnipresence and the Allness of God. It means that God is indeed All in All, the doer, the doing, and the deed, and one can say also the spectator. The Kingdom in this sense means all creation, on every plane, for that is the Presence of God—God as manifestation or expression.

The Power, of course, is the Power of God. We know that God is the only power, and so, when we work, as when we pray, it is really God doing it by means of us. Just as the pianist produces his music by means of, or through his fingers, so may mankind be thought of as the fingers of God. His is the Power. If, when you are praying, you hold the thought that it is really God who is working through you, your prayers will gain immeasurably in efficiency. Say, "God is inspiring me." If, when you have any ordinary thing to do, you hold the thought, "Divine Intelligence is working through me now," you will perform the most difficult tasks with astonishing success.

The wondrous change that comes over us as we gradually realize what the Omnipresence of God really means, transfigures every phase of our lives, turning sorrow into joy, age into youth, and dullness into light and life. This is the glory—and the glory which comes to us is, of course, God's too. And the bliss we know in that experience is still God Himself, who is knowing that bliss through us.

In recent years, the Lord's Prayer has often been rewritten in the affirmative form. In this style, for instance, the clause "Thy Kingdom come, thy will be done," becomes, "Thy kingdom is come, thy will is being done." All such paraphrases are interesting and suggestive, but their importance is not vital. The affirmative form of prayer should be used for all healing work, but it is only one form of prayer. Jesus used the invocatory form very often, though not always, and the frequent use of this form is essential to the growth of the soul. It is not to be confused with supplicatory prayer, in which the subject begs and whines to God as a slave pleading with his master. That is always wrong. The highest of all forms of prayer is true contemplation, in which the thought and the thinker become one. This is the Unity of the mystic, but it is rarely experienced in the earlier stages. Pray in whatever way you find easiest; for the easiest way is the best.

WITH GOD IN A DEVELOPING COUNTRY

Archbishop Emanuel Milingo

Prayer, for Archbishop Emanuel Milingo, is the heartbeat of the lover for the beloved, of the child for his Father. Through prayer comes the intense joy of being in the presence of the beloved.

His Eminence was born to a poor shepherd family. He received his education in Zambia, Rome, and Dublin. In 1969 he was consecrated by Pope Paul at Kampala, Uganda, as archbishop. Since 1965 he has been responsible for all religious broadcasting for the Catholic Church in Lusaka. He is also a founder of the Zambia Helpers Society movement, author of: "Communist Dialectics and Tactics in Developing Countries," "Patronado and Apartheid: Easter Message," and "Amace-Joni."

I want to speak to you about simple things. I am certain that you like to listen to simple things so that they can enter the mind quickly. But when I say that I am going to speak about "prayer," you might say, "But that is not a simple thing." Often in our catechism classes or during a sermon someone spoke to us about prayer in such a complicated way that we ended up by saying, "Prayer must be very difficult indeed!"

I consider prayer as a simple exercise. To me, prayer is a natural channel of communication between a creature and his Creator. When a creature feels life in him, when he sees a wonderful world around him, he cannot but start a conversation with the One who is the cause of it all. He likes to thank, to wonder, to enjoy, and to adore. He suddenly loves the One who made him part of all this beauty. That is why I would rather say: Prayer is the palpitation of the heart of the lover for the beloved. The beloved is never absent from the lover. He sees him, he talks with him, he wishes him well, and he is ashamed of any misdemeanor against him. That is why it is wrong to say that God is only with us when we are celebrating the Eucharist or when we enter a church. If God is truly my beloved, He is everywhere, wherever I am. He is with me and He accompanies me as the beloved.

May I reduce the nature of prayer to a still simpler example. Take the case of the lover and the beloved: the separation of the two does not change the power of their love for one another. The intensity of their love grows even more. They long to be together, and their imagination develops into pictures of possibilities, as to how he is now and where he might be; how he looks since I saw him last and how I should write him a love letter. Their longing for reunion grows from day to day. The separation of the lover from the beloved increases the fondness between them.

God, my dear brothers and sisters, is not separated from us, though we often think He is. In fact He is not far from us: He is with us, but in a form our poor minds are unable to perceive. His presence is felt by all those who really believe in Him. Just like the two blind friends, walking beside one another, supporting one another: though they do not see each other, they believe in and feel the presence of each other. In this way should every son and daughter of God feel His presence at all times—as he or she awakens, washes, goes to work, says his daily prayers, is busy with the children, or just walks around in the fields. God is not an uninterested spectator of our actions, but both the coach and the aim of our actions. He wants us to act as His sons and daughters should act. He anticipates the success of our actions and He rejoices when there is no disappointment. Prayer therefore is the palpitation of a child's loving heart for his Father, for God, the beloved.

Formal Prayer

Now, sometimes we hear the words "formal prayer." By this is meant our set prayers, which we recite so often: the rosary, the prayers during Mass, morning and evening prayers, and the prayer before meals. These are prayers everybody knows, and in times of great stress or when someone asks us to lead the prayers, we just start reciting an "Our Father" or "Hail Mary." But we must never forget that without the understanding of the true relation between the creature and the Creator, about which I spoke just now, this kind of formal prayer may become a habit and just a cold law, which we must obey. Often we do like the husband whose wife complained that he did not return from his work as quickly as he used to do and that his love was finished. He bought a tape recorder, filled a complete tape with the words "I love you, dear," and told his wife to play it when she felt lonely in the evenings. We must remember that we are lovers of God and everything we do must be the unfolding of that love to Him.

The formal prayers should be considered, in our African context, as "chewing the cud." That is to say, during formal prayer we "regrind" the spiritual food that is needed for ourselves and for all those we pray for. I think another example could be that formal prayer is an oasis, where we draw our strength and where we are always ready—after being refreshed—to start again. In this way we have to consider whether our actions have been as high as we expected or desired. If we have failed, we ask for pardon of God, who is the receiver of our actions. We talk with Him and ask advice as to how to proceed.

Importance of Prayer

"We should always pray." I wonder whether we have the same simple belief in this line that Saint Paul had. We cannot persevere in our apostolic work without prayer. We cannot share the benefits of our Faith with others unless we know how to pray. Throughout my years of pastoral work, I have been involved in social activities, which by themselves could have been sufficient to satisfy my ego. But I must confess that it often happened that I could not sleep till I had said my prayers. Never have I been so satisfied by carrying out projects of service to my fellow man that I found that this work actually replaced my personal prayer. I always felt that I had to go to the reference library, that is, to Jesus Christ Himself, the perfect Son of God, in order to sit with Him and to talk to our common Father. Though I believe in being recollected in God's presence, wherever I am, I still feel the importance of reserving a time exclusively for my Beloved. I enjoy being alone with Him, my Savior, who is the Truth, the Way and the Light.

"Teach Us How to Pray"

Now, you might ask me to show you some ways of prayer, of being with the Beloved. Again we must say that this is very simple. For me, one of the best ways is surely to sit with Him, to be with Him, and to relax completely in His presence. Prayer should be moments of intense joy, and we should not try to heap one word upon the other. "Come here and relax a bit," said Jesus to the Apostles, after a full day's work. Often we enter a church or a small room with many worries and many frustrations. We are angry with people and we are tired. But when we are just with Him, we should shake everything from ourselves as does a dog when it comes out of the water. Then we shall remain high and dry with Him. And we then realize that all these frustrations or worries or feelings of discontent come from our pride or from attempts to make our ego triumphant over others. In fact, we let ourselves fill with the warm love of Our Creator, while all the ill feelings toward our fellow men gurgle away into the waste. Coming away from such moments of intense silence before the Origin of All Good, we are as refreshed as if we had taken a cool bath in the clear river. We then notice that our attitude toward our fellow men has changed and taken the attitude of the loving God.

The Apostles, we know, asked the same question of Jesus: "Lord, teach us how to pray," and Jesus pronounced the wonderful words of the "Our Father." When we pray for something we should try to pray for the things which Jesus, Our Savior, prayed for: "May your kingdom come." Yes, may our prayer extend God's kingdom on earth: may His love be known.

Someone who loves and is loved wants to communicate his happiness to others. You know how it happens with a youngster. He might be very sulky and difficult, but one day he is just radiant and nice toward others. We then quickly say, "He must be in love," because you can almost read it in his face. So in our prayers we should want to communicate our love toward others: May your Kingdom come. May your love be felt by others. May they realize the happiness of being the sons and daughters of God. May they be with us, O Lord.

My dear brethren, God is not a punisher but a rewarder. To refer to punishment is the last thing that God will do. God is knocking on the door of our hearts, so often closed. When he speaks to us today, "let us listen to Him and let us not harden our hearts like stones." He sent His Son to redeem man, not to punish him. Sometimes we do sin, but honestly it is hard for me to imagine myself sinning outside God—without still remembering that I am His son. The temptations, the moral weaknesses, all these sufficiently help me to realize how weak I am by myself. Then I am obliged to look back to my God and He fills my hollow heart with Himself. The immensity of my sorrow for my sins will wipe away the dirt on my soul. God Himself uplifts me from the pitfall and once more helps me to walk again in His presence.

My brothers and sisters, may this genuine spirit of prayer be always with you.

MAN IS PRAYER

Archbishop Joseph Tawil

Archbishop Joseph Tawil finds in prayer the well of joy that encompasses praise, hope, repentance, and glory. His Excellency, the Titular Archbishop of Myra, is Apostolic Exarch for the Melkites in the United States. He has been director of the Patriarchal College, Cairo, and publisher of the patriarchal bulletin *Le Lien;* Patriarchal Vicar at Alexandria, Egypt; and Patriarchal Vicar at Damascus, Syria.

Prayer—A Constantly Renewed Joy: Prayer is not a pious occupation that is learned in books but an intimate and personal experience that no one can have in our place and that gives meaning to our whole life, to our entire existence. Man lives but once, and so it is of the utmost importance that he make of his life not a success or a triumph—that does not always depend on him and besides does not amount to much—but rather a wellspring of ever renewed joy.

Doxological Prayer (Prayer of Glorification): Why, as a matter of fact, should we not overflow with joy at the sight of so marvelous a world, made for our happiness and enchantment? How can man refrain from rejoicing at the idea that from the very moment of our creation we have been the object of God's loving kindness? Did not God place the first man in Eden? And didn't He converse with him at eventide as friend to friend? Like Adam[1] we discover anew every day this exhilarating world of wonders which reveals itself to us in its own language. Does not the smallest plant speak to us of God's grandeur, the least flower, of His beauty? Is not the slightest smile capable of throwing us into ecstasy at His infinite and exquisite goodness? Really, man has lost this sense of wonder before the beauty of the visible world. The hectic pace of life does not leave time to devote to contemplation and reflection. His whole life could be a "doxology" without end, praise and glorification of God, Who though unique in grandeur and dwelling in the highest heavens yet agrees to become a pilgrim for and with us, just as He did with the disciples at Emmaus:[2] accepting the invitation to share our table and by the Incarnation becoming one of us. Such is His intimacy with man.

For this reason, mirroring the shepherds who after having seen the Firstborn lying in the manger "returned, glorifying and praising God for all they had heard and seen" (Luke 2:20), the first cry to well up in our hearts, the first name which we ought to stammer, as a baby learning to talk, is the name of our heavenly Father, for He envelops us with His presence, with His love, with His glory. From all eternity He loved us, even before He formed us in our mother's womb.

The Great Sadness of Modern Man: Is it not the sense of wonder lacking in man that has caused him to turn in on himself, choking on his limitations and becoming the prey of sorrow? Who will deny man's great sadness? No matter how much, no matter how hard he tries to avoid it by sating himself with distractions, amusements, frivolities and pastimes, it pursues him

everywhere. You can even see the traces of sadness'
pursuit on his face. Man has cause for seeing everything
as dull and insipid beyond words. While he has received
the world from God's hands, he has turned away from
the Giver to cling to the gift, instead of returning it to
Him in "doxology," thanksgiving. Man has forgotten
that every perfect gift comes from the Father of Lights
to Whom he owes a debt of gratitude. That is why he is
held in thrall to so great a sadness which devours the little *joie de vivre* that he has left. Man forgets that he
does not live by bread alone but by every word that
comes from the mouth of God. Still this very sadness
can ripen into joy and become a gateway to salvation by
means of repentance. For God knows that we were
fashioned out of clay but He also knows that He has
imprinted His image on us. Even sin itself cannot destroy that image, for it is destined to eventual self-per-
fection until it achieves the Divine Likeness. Only then
does it reach its full measure, the fulfillment of the Gift
of Christ.

Prayer Billowing with Hope: Discouragement resulting from our miserable failures is the soul's worst af-
fliction. We have to recognize that despite the scars of
sin, "within us we bear the brilliance of His ineffable
glory."[3] Nor can we ever forget that God in His infinite
condescension has loved us despite our deficiencies precisely "in order to cause to shine on our faces the light
of His countenance."[4] In fact, couldn't we say that the
Creator fell in love with His creation to the point of giving it His only Son "so that whoever believes in Him
might not perish but have eternal life"?[5] Isn't this what
Saint Paul means when he speaks of the folly of the
Cross? So away with discouragement in face of our sins![6]
Let us adopt the attitude of Saint Isaac the Syrian: "All

the sins of mankind amount to but a grain of sand in the ocean of His love."

Renewed by the Tears of the Joy of Repentance: Of course, this ought not lead us to take sin lightly—that would be to tempt God—but ought rather to bring us to repentance of our faults, to a genuine conversion of heart and spirit to Him who alone is deserving of our love. How can it be that we do not fear that sin will forever separate us from that ocean of goodness and beauty? But such is the mystery of free will which enables man to lose God's friendship and to flounder on the rocks of his destruction. Thus Saint Isaac the Syrian offers as a definition of all prayer, "the quaking of the soul before the gates of Paradise." This explains the character of loving, confident repentance: as we abandon ourselves in the arms of the Father, no sooner does He hear the cry for forgiveness of His prodigal son than He throws His arms around him, presses him to His breast, covers him with kisses, and gives the order for festivities. Herein also lies the clearly paschal character of repentance, which can be defined as a "return to Paradise" at which the very angels of heaven rejoice.

The Spirit of the Father Prays in Us: It is the Spirit of the Father dwelling in us that makes us cry out, "Abba, Father," and this gives our prayer its validity. This same Spirit causes our hearts to flutter, the voice to well up in our throats, and our ears to perk up. He animates all our senses and grants understanding to our faculties and to our whole person.

Nothing can be done without Him; for it is He who renders our prayer efficacious. Thanks to Him it is transformed and drenches the world in a rain of graces.

Formerly, at the moment of ordination to the ministry, the deacon solemnly commanded the assembly to pay strict attention and to keep silent, because the

Spirit Who was being invoked was about to descend on the candidate for Holy Orders. This Spirit Whom we have received in baptism empowers us by His sanctifying might to receive in communion the Body and Blood of our Lord Jesus Christ into Whose Image we are transformed. Thus do we become the temple of the Holy Spirit and the members of the Body of Christ which is the Church. This same Spirit makes present the Risen Christ and manifests His power in the Church and the Sacraments. Finally it is He who brings history to its fulfillment because, since Pentecost, the world veers toward its end.

Seek First the Kingdom of God and His Justice: Prayer of petition constitutes the second objective of the Lord's Prayer and concerns our needs. For many it occupies the first place, since for them prayer means asking God to fulfill their needs. In reality we can and should do so, in the conviction that our heavenly Father knows our needs before we formulate them and grants us His grace before we even ask for it. We ought to seek first the Kingdom of God and His Justice and everything else will be added unto us.⁷ But God has a need for men: if He gives, it is, in fact, in order that we may give; if He has mercy on us, it is so that we may share in the misery of others. To do otherwise would be to enclose God's gift within the limits of our egotism and keep the waters of Grace from flowing.

Created for Glory: All prayer is the intimate experience of the discovery of God beginning with the signs and symbols of the language of creation wherein He is hidden. Since the Incarnation, God has a human face Who is the Christ, the Son of the Living God. "For we do not come to Him; it is rather He that inclines the heavens in search of us, and when He did not find Adam on earth He descended into Hell itself to free him

from his chains" to enable him to climb from the abyss
into which he had fallen from the bosom of the Glory of
the Father. If He asks us to carry His Cross, it is because He has destined us for glory, and it is not too
much to partake of His sufferings here below before entering His Kingdom, "for His commandments are not
burdensome" (John 5:3). And we know that "His yoke
is sweet and His burden is light" (Matt. 2:30) with the
assistance of His Grace, as He Himself assures us. And
His generosity is beyond imagining: He who knows
how to reward a glass of water given in His Name. For
when He rewards, He exceeds all hope, all expectations.
He crosses the frontiers of generosity; He knows no limits. He does it infinitely, divinely.

You Are Gods: The Image of God which He has imprinted on us must be polished to the point of completely reflecting the archetype. The polishing is brought
about by prayer and the sacraments of the Church, par-
ticularly by the Eucharist which plunges our entire being into the fire of Christ's divinity, making it become
fire in its turn. From the beginning man was promised
life with God, life in God, as Saint Peter says, "To
share in the divine Life."[9] Now what else does sharing
in the Divine Nature mean if not being deified? We will
be by participation what God is by nature. Plunged into
the fire iron becomes fire itself; but once removed from
the fire it becomes iron, or something else, once more.
Just as the firmament which receives the light of the
sun reflects and diffuses it, so it will be with the Just,
"who will shine like suns in the kingdom of their Father."[10]

Only when one has read the entire book can one
judge its contents; only when one has seen the film
through to the end can one judge its value. So it is with
each one of us: only at the end of one's life can one es-

timate its worth. Woven by the hand of the Divine Artist, it will unfold to bedazzled eyes the shimmering of the pearls of grace which have gained for us the Kingdom of Glory. To Him be glory and adoration, now and always and forever and ever!

[1] Gen. 3:8
[2] Luke 24:13
[3] Service for the Dead
[4] *Ibid.*
[5] John 3:15
[6] I Cor. 1:18
[7] Matt. 6:33
[8] Office of Holy Friday
[9] Peter 1:4
[10] Matt 13:43

NO TIME FOR GOD

Lubomyr Husar

Through prayer we acknowledge our dependence on God and express our convictions. But, notes Lubomyr Husar, in our preoccupation with our wordly business we are often so "busy" that we exclude the loving presence of God.

Lubomyr M. Husar, a native of Ukraine, received his licentiate in theology from the Catholic University of America in Washington, D.C. He engaged in pastoral ministry and teaching at the St. Basil's Ukrainian Seminary in Stamford, Conn. In 1967 he received his MA in philosophy from Fordham University, and in 1972 he received his STD at the Pontificia Universita Urbaniana in Rome. At present he is assistant professor of fundamental theology at that university. Father Husar is a monk of the St. Theodore Studite Monastery in Castel Gandolfo near Rome.

A friend of mine, a city pastor—a very active and wise administrator—suffered a heart attack. When he came to himself, he was a different man. He recovered his strength sufficiently to retain his pastorship, but his interests were no longer the same. Now he has time for prayer and the spiritual needs of his people. From a widely admired administrator of church property he has become a true pastor of his flock.

This happy metamorphosis—so he himself says—came over him as a result of his coming close to death. Somehow in the course of his near-fatal illness he understood that there is more to life than meets the eye. Man of himself is very weak, but engulfed in the love of His Creator and heavenly Father he is strong and secure. This understanding made the successful and certainly well-intentioned worldling into a man of God, a man of prayer, and a brother to his fellow men as he should have been all the time.

That story had a very happy ending. It repeats itself often enough, but its lesson, unfortunately, is usually restricted to the person involved. We others who did not undergo such a critical experience fail to see its implications for us.

It is no secret that most of us absolutely do not have the time for prayer. From morning till night we are caught up in various activities, all of which lay a just claim on our time. When we manage to snatch a free moment we have to relax—our health demands that from us. When vacation time comes around it is usually a hectic race from the minute we turn the key of our house door in good-by until, totally exhausted, we turn it again two or three weeks later. Vacation time, so precious and so short, is time free from all our normal engagements; consequently, free also from prayer, if such were our habit during our working days. There is, of course, Sunday, the official day of prayer. But how well observed? The prayer part is somehow submerged under all the social bustle.

Let us stop! Let us not wait for a heart attack to slow us down beyond repair. Why is it that we do not have time for prayer? Really, the chronic lack of time for prayer is only a symptom of an unhealthy state of mind.

Prayer is the conscious acknowledgment of our dependence on God expressed in some way. This description contains all the important elements of prayer. The fundamental truth from which prayer takes all its meaning is the fact of our dependence on God. We have been created; we do not exist of ourselves. There was a time when we were not; there will be a time when no trace of our existence on this earth will be left. We are a passing reality. Our existence is ultimately from God, Who alone exists through Himself and through no other. Not only we but the whole universe comes from the same hand of God. No matter how extensive it is, the same laws govern it, as our attempts to travel through space have so amply demonstrated.

Our dependence on God is totally peculiar. He Himself tells us that our relationship to Him is that of children to a father. He has chosen to set us into being, not as mineral stones, not as lovely plants, not as swift animals but as rational beings to whom He communicates Himself as a father to his children. This relationship, which men would never even presume to suspect, has been revealed to us by God Himself. He asks that we address Him as Father, and He in turn bountifully showers His gifts on us. The father-child character of the relationship that obtains between God and ourselves is of utmost importance for us. If it did not exist we still would have to admit our dependence but that would be a purely mechanical, totally impersonal, heartless, joyless affair. Even then we would be obligated by the sheer fact of our existence to acknowledge that we have taken our origin from some other, superior being. As things stand, however, we are children in a very real sense: God is our Father.

Every page of the sacred scriptures tells us of our heavenly Father. How is it possible that we overlook such a basic truth in our daily life? Obviously we do not read and meditate on God's revealed word. The life that we lead can easily distort our vision. All that we have and use is man-made. We hardly ever reflect that the finest things in life—as Mark Twain is said to have observed—sun, air, water and life, are given to us free. We take them completely for granted. We have learned to survive grave natural disasters, we have taken great strides into the universe, we are repeatedly made proud by new technological achievements. Our preachers and prophets often enough these days cater to our sense of pride. It is usually only when we come into a critical situation, not unlike that of my friend, that the whole truth begins to dawn on us: we are fragile creatures.

Once we come to realize our dependence on God we begin to pray. Prayer can take various forms—asking for favors, or begging forgiveness, or adoration unencumbered by any other sentiment. The form is not important. The central idea is that we as rational beings, creatures endowed with reason, knowingly and willingly acknowledge our dependence on God.

To this many people—I myself have met scores of them—say, of course, I know that God is my creator. But pray they do not. What is lacking? A realization that man must somehow give an expression to his convictions. Mere rational cognition does not suffice. Let's take a case like this: a young couple get married. The husband immediately goes away to another city where he can earn much more money, which he duly sends to his spouse. This is his way of loving and caring. Grateful as she may be for this, the woman has good grounds to wonder whether they are really a married couple. Does she have a husband? Legal documents and the financial support seem to prove it, but who would want such a life? True meaningful companionship is completely lacking. Similarly, the person who knows that God is his creator and sustainer but refuses or neglects to give that relationship its proper expression is somehow not living up to his belief.

To see better how prayer is an external expression of our dependence on God, let us take an example of a special kind of a religious act, a pilgrimage. Nowadays, a pilgrimage no longer entails many of the hardships of past days. We get into a car or bus, speed to our destination, spend several hours there, then hurry back. Generally not more than one day is spent and even that is spent in cushioned comfort. But even under these circumstances we perceive that two things which we prize very highly, time and money, have been spent to seemingly no good purpose. A person who does not believe in God would never "waste" his time and money in such a foolish way. To consider a one-week pilgrimage to Lourdes, let us say, surpasses even the imagination of "busy" people. What good, they ask, can come of it?

That same question is asked many times over when someone dares to suggest daily prayer. Are not the ten or five minutes better spent in learning something or recovering our strength for better effort in our normal work? The answer, of course, depends on our understanding of our existence. If we take ourselves as the ultimate reality, then no amount of persuasion or reasoning can succeed in making us pray. And logically so. The case is quite different if we permit our faith to set the tone of our lives. Then prayer becomes a necessity. The question in the long run is not how do I find time for prayer, but do I believe that God is my Father? We always find time for eating and sleeping—time is not the real problem.

What is the state of prayer to which we should aspire? Our Lord has told us to remain in prayer always. Is that possible? Yes, it certainly is. Must we then close ourselves into monasteries, and give up all work and activity? How few could do this, and yet the Gospel speaks to all, not just a chosen few. Have you ever considered a child at play? He seems to be completely preoccupied with his toys and games. He is, however, constantly conscious of his mother's presence. He lifts his head to look when she is leaving the room, no matter how quietly she may open the door. A feeling similar to that must be developed in regard to God. A person who meditates and reflects much on his relationship, on his dependence on God, and often turns his attention to his loving Father acquires a special sense for Him, a consciousness of God that does not cease.

THE GAME WITH MINUTES

Frank C. Laubach

Spiritual growth is a process of becoming increasingly close to God. Dr. Frank C. Laubach tells us how to abet that growth—how to practice the presence of God and find exhilaration, strength, and peace in bringing Him into every minute of our lives.

Dr. Laubach during his lifetime brought literacy programs to 103 countries and taught over 60 million people to read. He started in 1929 with the Moro tribesmen of the Philippines, when he translated their unwritten Magindanao language into a Roman alphabet. In a very short time, 70,000 Moros became literate. When the Depression forced the cutting of U.S. aid, the Moros continued teaching, using the "Each One Teach One" method. His work went beyond the field of literacy to that of the religious when he wrote *Prayer—the Mightiest Force in the World*. The Laubach Literacy Organization, which he founded before his death, is carrying on his "War of Amazing Love" against ignorance and poverty.

Christ Is the Only Hope of the World

"Disillusioned by all our other efforts, we now see that the only hope left for the human race is to become like Christ." That is the statement of a famous scientist, and is being repeated among ever more educators, statesmen, and philosophers. Yet Christ has not saved the world from its present terrifying dilemma. The reason is obvious: Few people are getting enough of Christ to save either themselves or the world. Take the United States, for example. Only a third of the population belongs to a Christian church. Less than half of this third attend service regularly. Preachers speak about Christ in perhaps one service in four—thirty minutes a month! Good sermons, many of them excellent, but too infrequent in presenting Christ.

Less than ten minutes a week given to thinking about Christ by one-sixth of the people is not saving our country or our world; for selfishness, greed, and hate are getting a thousand times that much thought. What a nation thinks about, that it is. We shall not become like Christ until we give Him more time. A teachers' college requires students to attend classes for twenty-five hours a week for three years. Could it prepare competent teachers or a law school prepare competent lawyers if they studied only ten minutes a week? Neither can Christ, and he never pretended that he could. To his disciples he said: "Come with me, walk with me, talk and listen to me, work and rest with me, eat and sleep with me, twenty-four hours a day for three years." That was their college course—"He chose them," the Bible says, "that they might be with him," 168 hours a week!

All who have tried that kind of abiding for a month know the power of it—it is like being born again from center to circumference. It absolutely changes every person who does it. And it will change the world that does it.

How can a man or woman take this course with Christ today? The answer is so simple a child can understand it. Indeed unless we "turn and become like children" we shall not succeed.

1. We have a study hour. We read and reread the life of Jesus recorded in the Gospels thoughtfully and prayerfully at least an hour a day. We find fresh ways and new translations, so that this reading will never be dull, but always stimulating and inspiring. Thus we walk with Jesus through Galilee by walking with Him through the pages of His earthly history.

2. We make Him our inseparable chum. We try to can win a high percentage of His minutes with as little do not need to forget other things nor stop our work, but we invite Him to share everything we do or say or think. Hundreds of people have experimented until they have found ways to let Him share every minute that they are awake. In fact, it is no harder to learn this new habit than to learn the touch system in typing, and in time one can win a high percentage of His minutes with as little effort as an expert needs to write a letter.

While these two practices take all our time, yet they do not take it from any good enterprise. They take Christ into that enterprise and make it more fruitful. They also keep a man's religion steady. If the temperature of a sick man rises and falls daily the doctor regards him as seriously ill. This is the case with religion. Not spiritual chills and fevers, but an abiding faith which gently presses the will toward Christ all day, is a sign of a healthy religion.

Practicing the presence of God is not on trial. It has already been proven by countless thousands of people. Indeed, the spiritual giants of all ages have known it. Christians who do it today become more fervent and beautiful and are tireless witnesses. Men and women who had been slaves of vices have been set free. Catholics and Protestants find this practicing the presence of

God at the heart of their faith. Conservatives and liberals agree that here is a reality they need. Letters from all parts of the world testify that in this game multitudes are turning defeat into victory and despair into joy.

Somebody may be saying, "All this is very orthodox and very ancient." It is indeed, the secret of the great saints of all ages. "Pray without ceasing," said Paul, "in everything make your wants known unto God." "As many as are led by the Spirit of God, these are the sons of God."

How We Win the Game With Minutes

Nobody is wholly satisfied with himself. Our lives are made up of lights and shadows, of some good days and many unsatisfactory days. We have learned that the good days and hours come when we are very close to Christ, and that the poor days come whenever we push Him out of our thoughts. Clearly, then, the way to a more consistent high level is to take Him into everything we do or say or think.

Experience has told us that good resolutions are not enough. We need to discipline our lives to an ordered regime. The "Game with Minutes" is a rather light-hearted name for such a regime in the realm of the spirit. It is a new name for something as old as Enoch, who "walked with God." It is a way of living which nearly everybody knows and nearly everybody has ignored. Students will at once recognize it as a fresh approach to Brother Lawrence's "Practice of the Presence of God."

We call this a "game" because it is a delightful experience and an exhilarating spiritual exercise; but we soon discover that it is far more than a game. Perhaps a better name for it would be "an exploratory expedition," because it opens out into what seems at first like a beautiful garden; then the garden widens into a country; and at last we realize that we are exploring a new world. This may sound like poetry, but it is not overstating what experience has shown us. Some people have compared it to getting out of a dark prison and beginning to LIVE. We still see the same world, yet it is not the same, for it has a new glorious color and a far deeper meaning. Thank God, this adventure is free for everybody, rich or poor, wise or ignorant, famous or unknown, with a good past or a bad—"Whosoever will, may come." The greatest thing in the world is for everybody!

You will find this just as easy and just as hard as forming any other habit. You have hitherto thought of God for only a few seconds or minutes a week, and He was out of your mind the rest of the time. Now you are attempting, like Brother Lawrence, to have God in mind each minute you are awake. Such drastic change in habit requires a real effort at the beginning.

Many of us find it very useful to have pictures of Christ where our eyes will fall on them every time we look around. A very happy hobby is to collect the most friendly pictures of Christ, pocket size, so that we can erect our own shrine in a few seconds.

How to Begin

Select a favorable hour; try how many minutes of the hour you can remember God at least ONCE each minute; that is to say, bring God to mind at least one second out of every sixty. It is not necessary to remember

God every second, for the mind runs along like a rapid stream from one idea to another.

Your score will be low at first, but keep trying, for it constantly becomes easier, and after a while is almost automatic. It follows the well-known laws of habit forming. If you try to write shorthand you are at first very awkward. This is true when you are learning to play a piano, or to ride a bicycle, or to use any new muscles. When you try this "game with minutes" you discover that spiritually you are still a very weak infant. A babe in the crib seizes upon everything at hand to pull himself to his feet, wobbles for a few seconds and falls exhausted. Then he tries again, each time standing a little longer than before. We are like that babe when we begin to try to keep God in mind. We need something to which we can cling. Our minds wobble and fall, then rise for a new effort. Each time we try we shall do better until at last we may be able to remember God as much as ninety per cent of the whole day.

How to Try the Experiment in Church

You have a good chance of starting well if you begin in church—provided the sermon is about God. When our congregation first tried it, we distributed slips of paper which read:

GAME WITH MINUTES
Score Card

During this hour I thought of God at least

once each minute for_____different minutes.

Signed _____

At the opening of the service the pastor made this announcement: "Everybody will be asked to fill in this score card at the end of one hour. In order to succeed, you may use any help within reach. You may look at the cross, or you may leaf through your hymn book or Bible, looking for the verses that remind you of God."

The sermon that Sunday explained how to play the game. At the end of the hour, the score cards were collected. The congregation reported scores ranging from five to sixty minutes. The average was forty-four minutes, which meant 73 per cent of the hour. For beginners this was excellent. Such an experiment, by the way, will encourage the congregation to listen better than usual, and will remind the preacher to keep his sermon close to God.

If you score 75 per cent in church, you can probably make a rather good score for the rest of the day. It is a question of being master of every new situation.

Never use a score card more than an hour, and not that long if it tires you. This is a new delight you are learning, and it must not be turned into a task.

While Going Home From Church

Can you win your game with minutes while passing people on the street? Yes! Experiments have revealed a sure way to succeed: offer a swift prayer for the people at whom you glance. It is easy to think an instantaneous prayer while looking people straight in the eye, and the way people smile back at you shows that they like it! This practice gives a surprising exhilaration, as you may prove for yourself. A half-hour spent walking and praying for all one meets, instead of tiring one, gives him a sense of ever heightening energy like a battery being charged. It is a tonic, a good way to overcome a tired feeling.

Some of us walk on the right side of the pavement, leaving room for our unseen Friend, whom we visualize walking by our side, and we engage in silent conversations with Him about the people we meet. For example, we may say: "Dear Companion, what can we do together for this man whom we are passing?" Then we whisper what we believe Christ would answer.

Where to Look for Christ

We have a right to use any aid that proves useful. One such aid is to think of Christ as in a definite location. To be sure, He is a spirit, everywhere at once—and therefore anywhere we realize Him to be. Many of us win our game nearly all of some days by realizing His unseen presence sitting in a chair or walking beside us. Some of us have gazed at our favorite picture of Him until it floats before our memories whenever we glance at His unseen presence, and we almost see Him. Indeed, many of us do see Him in our dreams. Others, like Saint Paul, like to feel Him within the breast; many, like Saint Patrick, feel Him all around us, above, below, before, behind, as though we walked in His kindly halo. We may have our secret ways of helping us to realize that He is very near and very dear.

On a Train or in a Crowd

We whisper "God" or "Jesus" or "Christ" constantly as we glance at every person near us. We try to see double, as Christ does—we see the person as he is and the

person Christ longs to make of him. Remarkable things
happen, until those in tune look around as though you
spoke—especially children. The atmosphere of a room
changes when a few people keep whispering to Him
about all the rest. Perhaps there is no finer ministry than
just to be in meetings or crowds, whispering "Jesus,"
and then helping people whenever you see an opportunity. When Dr. Chalmers answers the telephone he
whispers: "A child of God will now speak to me." We
can do that when anybody speaks to us.

If everybody in America would do the things just described above, we should have a "heaven below." This
is not pious poetry. We have seen what happens. Try it
during all this week, until a strange power develops
within you. As messages from England are broadcast in
Long Island for all America, so we can become spiritual
broadcasters for Christ. Every cell in our brain is an
electric battery which He can use to intensify what He
longs to say to people who are spiritually too deaf to
hear Him without our help.

While in Conversation

Suppose when you reach home you find a group of
friends engaged in ordinary conversation. Can you remember God at least once every minute? This is hard,
but we have found that we can be successful if we em-
ploy some reminders. Here are aids which have proven
useful:

1. Have a picture of Christ in front of you where you
can glance at it frequently.

2. Have an empty chair beside you and imagine that
your Unseen Master is sitting in it; if possible reach
your hand and touch that chair, as though holding His

hand. He is there, for He said: "Lo, I am with you always."

3. Keep humming to yourself a favorite prayer hymn —for example, "Have Thine Own Way, Lord, Have Thine Own Way."

4. Silently pray for each person in the circle.

5. Keep whispering inside: "Lord, put Thy thoughts in my mind. Tell me what to say."

6. Best of all, tell your companions about the "Game with Minutes." If they are interested, you will have no more trouble. You cannot keep God unless you give Him to others.

When at the Table

All the previous suggestions are useful at mealtime. If possible, have an empty chair for your Invisible Guest, who said, "Wherever two or three are gathered together, I am in the midst." Another useful aid is to recall what the Quakers believe about every meal. Jesus told us: "Eat this in remembrance of me." They think that He meant not only consecrated bread, but all food so that every mouthful is His "body broken for you."

While Reading a Book

When we are reading a newspaper or magazine or book, we read it to Him! We often glance at the empty chair where we visualize Him, or at His picture, and continue a running conversation with Him inwardly about the pages we are reading. Kagawa says scientific books are letters from God telling how He runs His universe.

Have you ever opened a letter and read it with Jesus, realizing that He smiles with us at the fun, rejoices with us in the successes, and weeps with us at life's tragedies? If not, you have missed one of life's sweetest experiences.

When Thinking

If you lean back and think about some problem deeply, how can you remember God? You can do it by forming a new habit. All thought employs silent words and is really conversation with your inner self. Instead of talking to yourself, you will now form the habit of talking to Christ. Many of us who have tried this have found that we think so much better that we never want to try to think without Him again. We are helped if we imagine Him sitting in a chair beside us, talking with us. We say with our tongue what we think Christ might say in reply to our questions. Thus we consult Christ about everything.

No practice we have ever found has held our thinking so uniformly high and wholesome as this making all thought a conversation with God. When evil thoughts of any kind come, we say, "Lord, these thoughts are not fit to discuss with Thee. Think Thy thoughts in my mind." The result is an instantaneous purification.

When Walking Alone

If you are strolling out of doors alone, you can recall God at least once every minute with no effort, if you remember that "beauty is the voice of God." Every flower and tree, river and lake, mountain and sunset, is God speaking. "This is my Father's world, and to my listening ears all nature sings." . . . "So as you look at each lovely thing, you may keep asking: 'Dear Father, what are you telling me through this, and this and this?' "

If you have wandered to a place where you can talk aloud without being overheard, you may speak to the Invisible Companion inside you or beside you. Ask Him what is most on His heart and then answer back aloud with your voice what you believe God would reply to you.

Of course we are not always sure whether we have guessed God's answer right, but it is surprising how much of the time we are very certain. It really is not necessary to be sure that our answer is right, for the answer is not the great thing—He is! God is infinitely more important than His advice or His gifts; indeed, He, Himself, is the great gift. The youth in love does not so much prize what his sweetheart may say or may give him, as the fact that she is his and that she is here. The most precious privilege in talking with God is this intimacy which we can have with Him. We may have a glorious succession of heavenly minutes. How foolish people are to lose life's most poignant joy, seeing it may be had while taking a walk alone!

But the most wonderful discovery of all is, to use the words of Saint Paul, "Christ liveth in me." He dwells in us, walks in our minds, reaches out through our hands, speaks with our voices, IF we obey His every whisper.

Be My Last Thought

We make sure that there is a picture of Christ, or a Bible, or a cross or some other object where it will meet our closing eyes as we fall asleep. We continue to whisper any words of endearment our hearts suggest. If all day long we have been walking with Him, we shall find Him the dear companion of our dreams. Sometimes after such a day, we have fallen asleep with our pillows wet from tears of joy, feeling His tender touch on our foreheads. Usually we feel no deep emotion, but always we have a "peace that passeth all understanding." This is the end of a perfect day.

Monday Morning

If on Sunday we have rated over fifty per cent in our game with minutes, we shall be eager to try the experiment during a busy Monday. As we open our eyes and see a picture of Christ on the wall, we may ask: "Now, Master, shall we get up?" Some of us whisper to Him our every thought about washing and dressing in the morning, about brushing our shoes and choosing our clothes. Christ is interested in every trifle, because He loves us more intimately than a mother loves her babe, or a lover his sweetheart, and is happy only when we share every question with Him.

Men at Work

Countless thousands of men keep God in mind while engaged in all types of work, mental or manual, and find that they are happier and get better results. Those who endure the most intolerable ordeals gain new strength when they realize that their Unseen Comrade is by their side. To be sure, no man whose business is harmful or whose methods are dishonest can expect God's partnership. But if an enterprise is useful, God eagerly shares in its real progress. The carpenter can do better work if he talks quietly to God about each task, as Jesus certainly did when He was a carpenter. Many of us have found that we can compose a letter or write a book better when we say: "God, think Thy thoughts in my mind. What dost Thou desire written? Here is my hand; use it. Pour Thy wisdom through my hand." Our thoughts flow faster, and what we write is better. God loves to be a coauthor!

Merchants and Bankers

A merchant who waits on his customers and prays for them at the same time wins their affection and their business. A salesman who prays for those with whom he is dealing has far more likelihood of making a sale. A bookkeeper or banker can whisper to God about every column of figures and be certain that God is even more interested in the figures than he is. The famous astronomer, Sir James Jeans, calls God the "super-mathematician of the universe, making constant use of mathematical formulae that would drive Einstein mad."

In the Home

Many women cultivate Christ's companionship while cooking, washing dishes, sweeping, sewing, and caring for children. Aids which they find helpful are:

1. Whispering to God about each small matter, knowing that He loves to help.

2. Humming or singing a favorite prayer hymn.

3. Showing the children how to play the game with minutes, and asking them to share in playing it. Chil-

dren love this game and develop an inner control when they play it which renders discipline almost needless.

4. Having pictures of Christ about the house, as a constant reminder.

5. Saying to God, "Think Thy thoughts in my mind."

When in School

An increasing army of students in school who are winning this game tell us how they do it. Here is their secret:

When in study period, say: "God, I have just forty precious minutes. Help my wavering thoughts to concentrate so that I may not waste a moment. Show me what is worth remembering in this first paragraph"— then read the lesson to God, instead of reading it to yourself.

When going to recitation, whisper: "Make my mind clear, so that I will be able to recall all I have studied. Take away fear."

When rising to recite before a group, say: "God, speak through my lips."

When taking an examination, say all during the hour, "Father, keep my mind clear, and help me to remember all that I have learned. How shall we answer this next question?" Visualize Him looking over your shoulder every minute you are writing. God will not tell you what you have never studied but He does sharpen your memory and take away your stage fright when you ask Him. Have you not discovered that when you pray about some forgotten name it often flashes into your memory?

To be sure, this prevents us from being dishonest or cheating, for if we are not honest we cannot expect His help. But that is a good reason for playing the game with minutes. Character is a hundred times more valuable than knowledge or high grades.

To be popular with the other students, acquire the habit of breathing a momentary prayer for each student you meet, and while you are in conversation with him. Some instinct tells him you are interested in his welfare and he likes you for it.

Praying Horseshoes

A very powerful way to pray is for a group of friends to join hands while seated in the shape of a horseshoe. Some of us have an altar at the open end of the horseshoe, with a cross or a picture of Jesus, or a Bible, or a globe of the world. The horseshoe opens toward the cities, countries, and people most in need of prayer.

This horseshoe of prayer reminds us of the great magnets which can lift a locomotive when the electric power is turned on. We are seeking to be used by the inpouring Holy Spirit to lift the world, and to draw all men to Christ.

It also reminds us of the radio broadcast which, when the power is on, leaps around the world. We offer ourselves as God's broadcasting station.

The gentle tingle which we usually feel reminds us of the glow and soft purr in the tubes of a radio when the power is on.

Every Christian family at mealtime may form a prayer radio broadcast by joining hands. Young people's societies will love it. It will vitalize every Sunday School class to spend ten minutes in broadcasting. Defunct prayer meetings will come to life when they become horseshoe magnets of prayer. Schools and colleges, public or private, will find prayer horseshoes popular with the students. Here is something that Christians and Jews can do together. Worship can thus be made the most thrilling experience of their lives.

The group may prepare a list of the most urgent world needs and of key persons. An excellent plan at breakfast is for someone to read from the newspaper the problems and persons which are most in need of prayer that morning.

The leader may say words like these: "Lord, in this terribly critical hour we want to do everything we can. We pray Thee, use us to help the President to be hungry for Thee, to listen and hear and obey Thee. We lift our President into Thy presence."

Then all may raise their clasped hands toward heaven. And so with the entire list.

After the prayer list is completed, the globe of the world may be lifted toward God while somebody prays the Lord's Prayer.

During Play Hours

God is interested in our fun as much as we are. Many of us talk to Him during our games. Some on the famous football players long ago discovered that they played better if they prayed all during the game. Some of the famous runners pray during races. If a thing brings health and joy and friendship and a fresh mind, God is keenly interested, because He is interested in us.

While on the playground, do not ask to win, but whisper: "God, get Thy will done exactly. Help us all to do our best. Give us what is far more important than defeating our opponents—make us clean sportsmen and make us good friends."

God and Love

Sweethearts who have been wise enough to share their love with God have found it incomparably more wonderful. Since "God is Love" He is in deepest sympathy with every fond whisper and look. Husbands and wives, too, give rapturous testimony of homes transformed by praying silently when together. In some cases where they had begun to give each other "nerves," they have found, after playing this game when they are alone together by day or by night, that their love grew strangely fresh, rich, beautiful, "like a new honeymoon." God is the maker of all true marriages, and He gives His highest joy to a man and wife who share their love for each other with Him, who pray inwardly each for the other when they are together looking into one another's eyes. Married love becomes infinitely more wonderful when Christ is the bond every minute and it grows sweeter as the years go by to the very last day. Imagine, too, what this does for the children!

Troubles

Troubles and pain come to those who practice God's presence, as they came to Jesus, but these seem trivial as compared to their new joyous experience. If we have spent our days with Him, we find that when earthquakes, fires, famines or other catastrophes threaten us, we are not terrified any more than Paul was in time of shipwreck. "Perfect love casteth out Fear."

The game with minutes is good for people suffering from illness at home or in hospitals. Nurses remind us that the thoughts of people turn toward God when sick as at no other time. Patients who are convalescing have many idle hours when their minds reach up toward God. Playing this game produces a perfect mental state for rapid recovery.

Those who are seeking to be aware of God constantly have found that their former horror at death has vanished. We may have a new mystic intimacy with our departed loved ones for though unseen to us, they are with Christ and since He is with us they are with us as well.

Some Prices We Must Pay to Win This Game

The first price is pressure of our wills, gentle but constant. What game is ever won without effort and concentration?

The second price is perseverance. A low score at the outset is not the least reason for discouragement; everybody gets a low score for a long while. Each week grows better and requires less strain.

The third price is perfect surrender. We lose Christ the moment our wills rebel. If we try to keep even a remote corner of life for self or evil, and refuse to let God rule us wholly, that small worm will spoil the entire fruit. We must be utterly sincere.

The fourth price is tell others. When anybody complains that he is losing the game, we flash this question back at him: "Are you telling your friends about it?" For you cannot keep Christ unless you give Him away.

The fifth price is to be in a group. We need the stimulus of a few intimate friends who exchange their experiences with us.

The Prizes We Win

It is obvious that this is unlike other games in many respects. One difference is that we all win. We may not win all or even half of our minutes but we do win a richer life, which is all that really matters. There are no losers excepting those who quit. Let us consider some of those prizes:

1. We develop what Thomas à Kempis calls a "familiar friendship with Jesus." Our Unseen Friend becomes dearer, closer and more wonderful every day until at last we know Him as "Jesus, lover of my soul" not only in songs, but in blissful experiences. Doubts vanish, we are more sure of Him being with us than of anybody else. This warm, ardent friendship ripens rapidly until people see its glory shining in our eyes—and it keeps on growing richer and more radiant every month.

2. All we undertake is done better and more smoothly. We have daily evidence that God helps our work, piling one proof upon another until we are sure of God, not from books or preachers, but from our own experience.

3. When we are playing this game our minds are pure as a mountain stream every moment.

4. The Bible and Christian hymns seem like different books, for they begin to sparkle with the beautiful thoughts of saints who have had glorious experiences with God. We begin to understand their bliss for we share it with them.

5. All day long we are contented, whatever our lot may be, for He is with us. "When Jesus goes with me, I'll go anywhere."

6. It becomes easy to tell others about Christ be-

cause our minds are flooded with Him. "Out of the fullness of the heart the mouth speaketh."

7. Grudges, jealousies, hatred, and prejudices melt
away. Little hells turn into little heavens. Communities
have been transformed where this game was introduced.
Love rises like a kindly sea and at last drowns all the
demons of malice and selfishness. Then we see that the
only hope for this insane world is to persuade people to
"practice the presence of God."

8. "Genius is ninety per cent concentration." This
game, like all concentration upon one objective, eventually results in flashes of new brilliant thought which as-
tonish us, and keep us tiptoe with expectancy for the
next vision which God will give us.

Infinite Variety

The notion that religion is dull, stupid and sleepy is
abhorrent to God, for He has created infinite variety
and He loves to surprise us. If you are weary of some
sleepy form of devotion, probably God is as weary of it
as you are. Shake out of it, and approach Him in one of
the countless fresh directions. When our minds lose the
edge of their zest, let us shift to another form of fellowship as we turn the dial of a radio. Every tree, every
cloud, every bird, every orchestra, every child, every
city, every soap bubble is alive with God to those who
know His language.

It Is for Anybody

Humble folk often believe that walking with God is
above their heads, or that they may "lose a good time"

if they share all their joys with God. What tragic misunderstanding, to regard Him as a killer of happiness! A growing chorus of joyous voices round the world fairly sing that spending their hours with God is the most thrilling joy ever known, and that beside it a baseball game or a horse race is stupid.

Radiant Religion

This game is not a grim duty. Nobody need play it unless he seeks richer life. It is a delightful privilege. If you forget to play it for minutes or hours or days, do not groan or repent, but begin anew with a smile. It is a thrilling joy—don't turn it into a sourfaced penance. With God, every minute can be a fresh beginning. Ahead of you lie limitless anticipations. Walt Whitman looked up into the starry skies and fairly shouted:

> "Away, O Soul, hoist instantly the Sail!
> O daring joy but safe!
> Are they not all the seas of God?
> O farther, farther, farther sail!"

What Is Meant by Winning

You win your minute if during that minute you either:
1. Pray.
2. Recall God.
3. Sing or hum a devotional hymn.
4. Talk or write about God.
5. Seek to relieve suffering of any kind in a prayerful spirit.

6. Work with the consciousness of God's presence.
7. Whisper to God.
8. Feel yourself encompassed by God.
9. Look at a picture or a symbol of Christ.
10. Read a scripture verse or poem about God.
11. Give somebody a helping hand for the Lord's sake.
12. Breathe a prayer for the people you meet.
13. Follow the leading of the Inner Voice.
14. Plan or work for the Kingdom of God.
15. Testify to others about God, the church, or this game.
16. Share suffering or sorrow with another.
17. Hear God and see Him in flowers, trees, water, hills, sky.

We never attempt to keep a minute-by-minute record (excepting perhaps occasionally for an hour), since such a record would interfere with normal life. We are practicing a new freedom, not a new bondage. We must not get so tied down to score-keeping that we lose the glory of it, and its spontaneity. We fix our eyes upon Jesus, not upon a clock.

THE MEANING OF PRAYER

Archbishop Michael Ramsey

We must submit our wills to God, declares Archbishop Michael Ramsey, so that through our good actions and prayers we may become the channels of God's goodness. Moreover, our prayers become ultimate assertions of the God/man relationship.

His Grace was educated at Repton, Magdalene, and Cuddesdon Theological College. He is a world traveler in the support of the Anglican Communion and ecumenical movement throughout the Americas, Asia, Africa, and Europe. He is a noted lecturer and author and was the chairman of the National Committee of Commonwealth Immigrants. Dr. Ramsey holds over fourteen honorary degrees from some of the most prominent colleges and universities in the world. Presently, he is the Archbishop of Canterbury.

Prayer is not a kind of pious chatter—indeed it is neither pious nor chatter—but a realizing of ourselves and God in right relation.

Let me first clear away some debris from our path: misleading ideas. One of the most misleading ideas is that prayer is a sort of bombardment. We want certain things for ourselves or for others, and so we bombard God with requests for what we want, sometimes with the idea that if a lot of us keep up the bombardment simultaneously something will happen. And when the result does not happen as we had hoped, we can be very disillusioned. The trouble was that the exercise started with ourselves and our own wishes—even though our wishes might be partly right—and also that this image of a bombardment suggests that God is some distance away from us, a kind of target away across the fields.

No, prayer is God and ourselves: near, together, sharing, conversing. An analogy: If it is your father or mother and you, or some great friend and you, the relationship is far deeper than one of you asking for things and the other saying "yes" or "no." The relation is one of being together, enjoying, loving, listening, talking, thinking, receiving the whole impress which passes from one to the other and back again. Something like that is the relation of God and ourselves, which is what prayer means.

Now you may react. You may say: "Oh, but I don't feel God to be near like that, I just don't get the sort of religious feeling which some people get; the prayers and hymns and all that; to me it is just blank."

Well, leave out any idea of feeling pious; no one wants you to feel pious. Leave out the word *God,* if you like. It is you, and the realities you know. Deep down in you there is a sense perhaps of tremendous obligation, things which are a "must" for you because they are right. So, too, in the lives of others there are things which you admire tremendously, with reverence and awe. Then, from time to time there is the horrid sense of guilt: something I am meant to be and I have willfully failed to be. Then in some of the crises of the world you remember a conviction in you that something is right and is therefore meant to prevail. And with all these experiences there is often a sense of wonder, wonder at something, someone, intimate with you in the depths of your being, and yet beyond, far beyond. It is all this which, for me, adds up to the word *God,* especially when I consider the person of Jesus as gathering up the whole. But perhaps for you, though it all means so much to you, though the heart of the matter is in you, there is a kind of emptiness, a blank, a hunger.

Now, it is just this emptiness, blank, hunger which can find any of us nearer to God than a spate of consciously religious feelings and phrases can. No one is nearer to God than the man who has a hunger, a want —however tiny and inarticulate. And that is where prayer can begin, the prayer of simply being oneself in utter sincerity. One can pray like this: "O my God, I want thee, help me to want thee more." "O my God, I love thee so little, help me to love thee as thou lovest me." "O my God, I scarcely believe in thee, increase my tiny faith." "O my God, I do not really feel sorry for my sin: but I want to, give me a true sorrow for it."

We don't find God by trying to be more religious than we are or can be. No, we are near God by being true to ourselves in all the experiences such as I described just now, and then God can begin to find us, to fill our emptiness, and some of the old phrases of religion can be near to what is in the heart.

"O Lord, thou hast searched me out and known me." "Whither shall I go then from thy presence?" God finding me.

"Make me a clean heart, O God." God making me fit to be near him.

"O God, thou art my God, early will I seek thee." Wanting God more than you ever thought you did.

"Praise the Lord, O my soul, and all that is within me, praise his holy name." Being grateful for all this and wanting to say how grateful you are.

Twenty years ago Dietrich Bonhoeffer, a pastor of the Lutheran Church in Germany, was put to death by the Nazis. Many years hence his *Letters from Prison* are, I think, likely to be read as a classic of Christian faith and spirituality. In his loneliness and privation, he found that God was there. He reacted against much of the religion of his time, but many of the letters show him still drawing upon psalms, hymns, and prayers—the old language of religion.

We were using the analogy of ourselves and a friend conversing. God is the friend of Man, and in any exchange between God and Man, God will be the one who is giving far more, giving so much that what Man gives seems feeble, tiny, almost nothing. It is God who searches, finds, gives, and what he gives is himself. That is the meaning of Christmas, Good Friday, Easter— God giving himself in generous self-giving to mankind, so that he is near us, with us, in us in ways beyond our imagining. God and us; yes, God and us together, and together in a wonderful nearness. And when we pray we will not be bombarding God with our own desires. We will be starting far nearer to God, sharing a little of his heart and mind, and putting our will at his disposal to serve his good purpose to the world.

I said earlier that prayer doesn't mean bombarding God with requests. If we think of it like that we are putting God wrongly at a distance from us like a target across the fields, and are starting with our own wills. No, prayer is a kind of intercourse between God and ourselves, ourselves and God, in which we soak our minds and hearts and wills in his, and so put ourselves at his disposal to become channels of his loving purposes towards the world, towards this or that person or affair.

But how do we soak ourselves in God's heart and

mind? It is like the overwhelming impact of person upon person when two are together, listening, loving, pondering, assimilating. Now this can be put in religious language, the language of psalm and hymn and devotion. Perhaps you find that language unreal to you and are shy of it. Very well, do not force yourself into it. And yet there may be ways in which, haltingly, inarticulately, you find God real to you; in the sense of supreme moral obligation which you sometimes feel; in the reverence of lovely qualities in people which seem to be somehow beyond and to give meaning to human existence; in the sense of guilt; in the sense of wonder at the world and its meaning. There you find the reality which has the name of God. But, just because he is supreme and majestic and you are not, it is not you finding him so much as he finding you. "Before I sought thee, thou didst find me."

It is this which Christianity puts into words of religion. God made the world, God made man in his own likeness, God is the giver of all good, and because God is the giver he gives no less a gift than himself to us. That is the meaning of Christmas, Good Friday, Easter. That is the center of our gratitude. And what would be just gratitude if it were between one man and another man, between a creature and a fellow creature, becomes praise, adoration, worship when it is between us who are creatures and sinners and one who is our Creator and our God. Worship means a kind of self-forgetfulness as we lose ourselves in praise and wonder, ascribing nothing to ourselves and all to him the good giver.

Now prayer. Our starting place is not our own will, but God. We find ourselves with him, so to speak, or rather realize he is near to us. And in our own words, or the words of the Bible, or other words given to us by Christians, or in no words, we praise, thank, wonder, love, confess sorrow for our sins, lift up our heart to God. We may specially dwell upon the image of God given to us in the story of Jesus, reading, seeing, reflecting: Jesus the image of the unseen God. So we are drawn inside the heart, the mind, the purpose of God. Our wills can begin to be attuned to his.

Now God's purpose is like a stream of goodness flowing out into the world and all its needs. But it is our privilege as God's children to help this stream of goodness to reach other people, becoming ourselves like channels. Our good actions can be channels of God's goodness, and so too can our prayers. We do not bombard God with our desires; no, we bring our desires into tune with his, so that he, waiting upon our cooperation and using the channel of our prayers, brings the stream of his good purpose into the parched deserts of human need.

Isn't this what Jesus tells us when he gives us the "Our Father" as the model prayer? Jesus meant not only "pray in these words," but "pray with this sequence of thought and desire." God first, the Father, the heavenly Father, hallowed be thy name. His name is his character and glory, to be dwelt upon, honoured, loved, our hearts and minds to be soaked in it. And then, we ask that his reign may come and his will be done. With our wills first surrendered to his we bring the affairs of the world to him in our requests.

There is in all of us a genuine freedom of will, and that freedom of will is the condition of a moral universe, a universe of moral beings and not automata.

Palm Sunday is the beginning of the week when Christians everywhere commemorate the crucifixion of Jesus. Its significance rests upon the belief that Jesus was, and is, divine, and that the event is a universal symbol of the conflict between the self-giving love of

God and the deep pride and selfishness which is in man.
Seen in the historical event, the conflict could know no
compromise. The selfishness of man, resisting and hating the self-giving love of God, destroyed Jesus by crucifixion. But there was another side to the story. The
self-giving love of God on its part cannot tolerate the
selfishness of man and sets out to destroy it—by the
only weapon which can destroy it, namely love itself.
The event is thus a symbol; more than that, it is an en-
actment of God's love invading the life of the world. It
is to that love that we try to submit our wills to become
its channels in our deeds and our prayers.

Prayer means God and us, near, together, conversing,
so that our mind and heart become filled with God's desires and purposes. Then, submitting our desires to
God's, we become a sort of channel of his good purpose
towards humanity and its needs.

So the Christian in his prayers, and his actions, is
looking constantly towards the world and its needs, and
looking with something of God's own care and love. In
that way we serve and love humanity, here, now. But
there is another aspect of the matter. The God and man
relation exists because our existence is intrinsically
concerned with God. Each one of us is his child and
creature. He created us in order that we might have a
fellowship with him lasting forever, with heaven as its
goal. That is the deep, lasting meaning of the God and
man relation.

Think how this is so. Each of us is created in God's
own image, and it means that though you are a creature
and full of sins and defects there is a deep-down likeness between us and God, and your destiny is to be
with him. When we say that God loves us we mean that
he cares for each single one of us as if there is no one
else for him to care for; he cares for you in all that

unique individuality which is yours. He wants you, to be
with him, forever, to share with you all he has to share.
That is heaven. It is the perfection of the God and man
relation. And it cannot be selfish in any way, because it
implies the plural, and heaven includes the mutual love
and service of all who share it together, a love and service totally integrated with the love of God and the vision of God.

If that is our goal, how does it affect our present daily
existence? In this way: Our prayer, while it is a channel
of God's good purposes in the world around, is also the
assertion of that God and man relation which has heav-
en as its goal. Indeed it is already a little anticipation of
heaven in the present life. And it is a good thing for the
world that this is so. It is good that there should be in
the midst of all this world's work and turmoil men and
women who love and serve humanity with their hearts
set upon that goal of heaven which is God's final purpose for every one of us.

Easter Sunday is the day when we commemorate the
Resurrection of Jesus. I recall a painting of the Risen
Christ by Piero della Francesca which has been called
"a monument of contemplation, in which the current of
life seems to flow with the deliberation of eternity." For
the Resurrection is an event which confirms and sets its
seal upon the belief of which we have just been thinking: that the goal of men is fellowship with God for
eternity. That is the meaning of our infinite worth to
God, and of those longings which we express, sometimes in words or religion and sometimes in a hunger
that finds no words at all, because God made us for
himself and our heart is restless until it finds rest in him.

PRAYING FOR ONE ANOTHER

Paul L. Higgins

In this selection Paul L. Higgins explores the
power of intercessory prayer—both the objective
good that comes to others and the subjective value
to the person of faith who prays for others.

Reverend Higgins, a minister of the United
Methodist Church and cofounder and first president of Spiritual Frontiers Fellowship, has served
pastorates in California and Illinois, including nine
years at Hyde Park, Chicago, and twelve years at
Richards Street Church in Joliet. A devotee of the
Christian mystical tradition, he conducts religious
retreats and seminars, and lectures on psychical
and spiritual subjects. He is the author of several
books, including *Preachers of Power, John Wesley: Spiritual Witness, Encountering the Unseen,*
and *Mother of All,* and is a contributor to an-
thologies, magazines and journals. He resides in
Rockport, Mass., and is the Founder-Director of
the Rockport Colony.

In our Christian heritage the power of intercessory
prayer is clearly expressed. Effective prayer is being in
communion with the all-powerful and all-merciful God,
who hears the requests of the faithful, and who answers
according to His good and perfect will.

Saint James writes in the New Testament, saying: "If any is afflicted, let him pray. If any is merry, let him sing psalms and be thankful. If any is sick, let him call for the elders of the Church, that they might come, pray over him, and anoint him with oil in the name of the Lord." Then he says that the prayer of faith shall heal the sick. If he has committed sins, he shall be forgiven. "Pray one for another, that ye may be healed. The effectual fervent prayer of a righteous man availeth much."

The effectiveness of prayer is discovered through our practice of prayer. The proof we find is in the individual experience of those who pray. As Martin Luther said: "None can believe how powerful prayer is, and what it is able to effect, but those who have learned it by experience."

Dr. Alexis Carrel, the French physician and surgeon, who later became famous for his discoveries in physiology and medicine and became a Nobel Prize winner, had a patient in his earlier years who was apparently dying. There was nothing more he could do for her. She wanted to go to the Shrine of Our Lady at Lourdes. Dr. Carrel was skeptical about religion at that time, but being a kind man, he accompanied her. He later confessed that as they approached the Shrine, he wondered in his heart what would happen in his own life if she should be cured. The young woman was healed almost immediately, in one of the miracles of faith. Dr. Carrel's life was changed; he always counted this experience the most important in his whole life. He became a man of great faith, and one of the modern world's greatest exponents of the prayer life.

Intercessory prayer has both subjective and objective values. The main purpose, of course, is objective; that is, to be of help to someone else. But a word should be

said for the subjective value, too. It has been said that
you cannot really hate another person when you begin
to pray for him. William Law, the English mystic, tells
the story of Susurrus, a pious man who had one serious
fault—he loved to gossip. One day he whispered some
choice bit of gossip into the ear of a friend. The latter
told him he should go home at once, and pray for the
man about whom he was spreading a tale. Susurrus was
upset by this advice but went home and prayed for the
man. He was never the same again. His heart was
changed, and he promised God he would never again
gossip; in fact, he named one day a week as a day of
penance, to confess his sorrow to God over his former
guilt. He kept the weekly day of penance the rest of his
life.

The grand value of intercession is the objective good
that actually comes to the lives of those for whom we
pray. Intercessory prayer is far more powerful than
most of us ever dream possible. As Gerald Heard says,
"It is good we do not always know how widespread is
the influence of our prayers, lest we become too proud
in the good that is accomplished."

"Pray one for another that ye may be healed." This is
to pray for the wholeness of the individual, that in mind
and body and soul, he might be what God wants him to
be. We are reminded how Our Lord Jesus set the example and told His disciples to do likewise, and how Peter
and Paul and John and James healed great numbers of
every type of sickness. The Apostles knew, as we know,
that not everyone is healed—at least not in the way expected. For Christians, death comes not as something to
be dreaded, but as an opening door to perfect healing
and everlasting life. As Christians, our task is to do as
Jesus commands us, to pray for the healing of the sick,

and to pray for the welfare and salvation of others, leaving the results in the hands of God.

The power released through prayer groups is greater than any realize. Good always comes from such prayers, sometimes in terms of miraculous results, sometimes gradually, and very often not noticeable at the time. But always good.

One day I called on a parishioner who was critically ill. Her doctor said he could do no more for her, and doubted whether she could live many months. This parishioner was concerned over her granddaughter, who was in trouble, and asked me if we would pray that she might live long enough to see the girl through her difficulty to the right path. I said we would pray both for her prayer request and for her healing. Our prayer group got to work. We prayed, believing God would hear and answer our prayers. Not only did the parishioner live to see her granddaughter out of trouble and restored to the right path, but the woman herself was healed, and is alive today, ten years later.

Sometimes, of course, those for whom we pray that they might be healed, die. We all must die, and with death inherit eternal life, and we must keep this larger perspective amid all of our prayers. But our task and duty is to pray affirmatively for healing, trusting completely in the wisdom of our God. God can cure incurable diseases, if it be His will. As the angel said to the Blessed Virgin: "With God, nothing is impossible."

I believe, completely and without reservation, that God hears our every prayer, and that He answers us always. Sometimes the answer is obvious to all. Other times, only a few can discern it, and sometimes no one seems aware of it, but we know within us that the blessing has come. It is important to maintain an affirmative mind, strong in faith, and receptive in heart and soul. I think that sometimes the very negativeness of thought and attitude on the part of friends and members of the family hinders the recovery of sick persons. When we pray, we must pray believing in the presence and power and goodness of God.

There are several questions people often ask regarding intercessory prayers.

In answering prayer, does God act contrary to laws of nature? The laws of nature are made by God. We know only a very few of them and these only in a fragmentary way. God acts according to His wisdom, power, and goodness, all of which far transcend our concepts and the few partial laws we may know.

Do our prayers actually influence God? If God is all-powerful, and knows all things, does He not act without our prayers? The Christian faith holds that our prayers do influence God. In some realms, wherein God has given us a measure of freedom, He does not act until we pray. In other realms, of course, He acts without our prayers.

God tells us in the Bible to pray, and makes it evident that He waits for our response to Him. John Wesley says in reference to the realms wherein we are given freedom, that "God does nothing but in answer to prayer. . . . Every new victory that a soul gains is the effect of a new prayer." Karl Barth, the theologian, says that "God does not act in the same way whether we pray or not. Prayer exerts an influence upon God's action . . ."

We are all linked together at certain levels, and as a social community, share in some measure each other's joys and woes. If we do not care enough for each other and for our common good to pray, then we suffer the consequences, individually and collectively. When we care enough to pray, a blessing comes to us and to oth-

ers in a measure not otherwise possible. Our very intercession plays a part in the redemption of the world. It is
what our Sovereign God expects of us.

*Are the prayers of some persons more effective than
those of others?* The Biblical answer is in the affirmative. As Saint James writes, "The prayer of faith shall
save the sick." The man of faith, the man who is righteous and who prays with all his heart and soul, *believing,* that man's prayer is powerful. To mumble words,
not half-believing what you say, obviously is not very
effective.

It is the prayer that grows out of real faith in Christ
that is truly effective. It is this, coming with all one's
heart and soul, that can be the greatest single factor,
and often the only factor, in the healing of the sick, in
the making of the good life, and in the building of a
good world, even a world of peace.

*Should we pray for the departed, and do they pray
for us?* Our God is the God of this world and all worlds,
of this level and all levels of life. We should pray for
one another here and for those who have departed this
life, that the latter may find joy and fulfillment in the
eternal world.

The Church includes the Church Militant and the
Church Triumphant, and to pray for each other in the
Church is to participate in the communion of saints.
Even as Saint John tells us in the Book of Revelation,
the saints in glory pray for us. The more we grow in the
spiritual life, the more wondrously real is the experience
of knowing that there are those dear and holy ones
across the line who are praying for us.

God grant that we might more and more enter into
the great spiritual blessedness of praying for one another. In our own intercession, let us remember all who are
sick in body or mind, or in conscience or soul. Let us

pray for the broken, for the penitent. Let us pray for a
new spirit of peace in the hearts of men. Let us pray for
the spiritual renewal of all people.

May we pray for one another with faith, with fervor,
and out of sincere and compassionate and truthful
hearts. And the grace of our Lord Jesus Christ will be
with us all, both now and always.

PRAYER-THERAPY

William R. Parker

Such personality characteristics as inferiority feelings, fear, guilt, and hate are impediments to a harmonious relationship between our inner self and our perception of the outer world. Dr. William R. Parker examines these characteristics and shows how prayer and meditation can restore this spiritual harmony.

Dr. Parker is a noted author, a psychologist and former professor of psychology at the University of Redlands, California. He is a lecturer and is a recognized authority in the area of prayer-therapy. His famous book *Prayer Can Change Your Life* is the basis for the prayer-therapy program. After working with patients who have psychosomatic problems, Dr. Parker is now in private practice in Newport Beach, California.

How can we use prayer and meditation for healing, for peace of mind and to identify with the Creative Force which is the source of all life? Let us approach it from the following four points of departure: (1) Make Prayer a Dialogue, (2) Make Prayer Positive, (3) Make Prayer a Practice in Honesty, and (4) Make Prayer a Regular Activity.

Make Prayer a Dialogue

The human personality is a dual personality that consists of an infantile portion and an adult portion. This is because maturity takes place in the cortex. When the infantile portion (the thalmus) is over-exhibited, we sometimes say to ourselves: "Why don't I grow up?" This may be an empty monologue—an ineffective prayer. Effective prayer needs to be a dialogue—a talking and listening. It seems to me that the basic reason most prayers are a monologue is that we have been taught, and the majority believe, that God is somewhere in outer space, that we talk to God "out there." Further, we have been taught that God is a person—an anthropomorphic god. The opposite is true; God is not isolated from man. God is in the midst of creation, of creativeness. God is Creativeness. God is Spirit. God is Love. Therefore, if we pray *to* God we imply separation, but if we pray *with* God, this implies integration, oneness, wholeness, unity.

Effective prayer is dependent upon our premises— our ground for understanding. Some of our premises are fearful, some are simply mouthing old concepts we have been taught or heard. Many have a premise that God is a judge, that one is punished from outside. Countless millions make the premise that they are helpless children in the face of an all-powerful God, and under the guise of making themselves humble, they attempt to make themselves small and, invariably, supplicate, plead, beg and beseech in their prayers. They begin to feel helpless and have little command over their lives. If, now, they would make prayer a dialogue their life and being could begin to change. By talking and identifying with the creative force within, they could begin to sense that they were made in this image and change their self-image to one based on self-acceptance. Self-acceptance is the single most important characteristic of our development. When we begin to appreciate that we are a part of the creative power of the universe, we begin to know that nothing is impossible.

Through dialogue we can be lifted into a state of feeling—a state of love, joy and peace. Then, we are able to listen to the great promptings from within—from God.

By surrendering our inner selves, we stop regarding influence, power and causation as arising from outside ourselves. We begin to realize that, essentially, the power for good or evil comes from within. Our *new* inner thought will not, actually, change the world, but it will change the world *for us*. It will not change for us if we only think other thoughts; we must do other deeds; we must change our behavior. ("Go and sin no more.")

What can we do? We can stop blaming other people and situations for our mistakes and adopt a new, dynamic attitude toward life. We can stop regretting past mistakes and select a worthy goal to move toward. We can see that we reap as we sow and that we can sow and reap anew. By becoming more aware of the detrimental aspects within us, we can escape reaping inferiority, fear, guilt and hate. They are detrimental to our personal well-being and our way of life. It is a law: the universe will give back action for action. It is clear, then, that we sow from within. We can listen and sow more wisely. We can make prayer a dialogue.

Make Prayer Positive

Positive prayer is not just wishful thinking nor being unrealistic and naive. Positive prayer becomes meditation at the point it becomes receptive. As it moves into meditation our prayer becomes an affirmation. Notice how receptive the following affirmation becomes: "So, in thought and deed, we gather up all mankind and hold them in the light, so there might be a benediction on every soul sincerely seeking to do justly, to love mercy, and to walk humbly with his God. We visualize ourselves becoming citizens of the universe."

Great prayer is not begging but affirming. We, invariably, act, feel and perform in accordance with what we imagine to be true about ourselves and our environment. It is, truly, done unto us as we believe. If we do not enjoy suffering, we can change the course of our lives. We do not make things happen; we allow them to happen. Effective prayer, then, is a process, a development.

With the development of the computer, which is an extension of man's brain, we know more about programming ourselves. Our subconscious is the computer part of our brain. What we do in our lives has been programmed into our subconscious. Some of this programming is negative or detrimental. However, we can *reprogram* ourselves at any time.

The memories stored in our subconscious are essentially visual and aural impulses—that is, sight and hearing. These two senses make the greatest imprint. Through new and positive affirmations, and creative and healing visualizations in our prayer life, the whole subconscious can be altered for the better. Let me give

a short example of a meditation that uses the positive
concept with the visualization that is necessary for
change, renewal and healing:

"We now become still. In the quietness, we sense that
there is one force, one spirit, one presence, one power
and this is of God. It surrounds us and permeates our
being. This force is Spirit—this power is all good. We
now identify with it and release it in our being.

"We sense a feeling of freshness—of newness—and
know that this is the first day of the rest of our lives. We
celebrate life and continually restore our health, our
harmony and peace in forgiveness and love. As we live
in this presence, our hearts are restored and we feel at
peace. We now select someone we love and we hold
them in the light—the healing light—the light of love.
We visualize this white light surrounding them and fill-
ing them. It permeates their whole being. We know they
are rejuvenated, renewed, refreshed and set free. We
see them happy, well, radiant of spirit, vital and ener-
getic.

"We simply say, 'Thank you, Father, Creative Spirit,
for all our gifts. We, too, have retreated to the moun-
tain-top of meditation, alone, and discovered we are not
alone. And so it is. Amen.' "

Positive prayer is not an escape from life. There is a
vast difference between *escape* and *losing oneself*. We
lose ourselves in the good, the true and the beautiful.
We give energy to our strengths, not to our weaknesses.
Erich Fromm has stated that: "Love is based on an attitude of affirmation and respect, and if this attitude does
not exist toward oneself, who is after all only another
human being and another neighbor, it does not exist at
all."

Through positive prayer and meditation, the negative
and fearful personalities can be "born again." Those

who lack good mental health can, through creative meditation, be transformed by the renewing of their minds. They can grow up again emotionally.

Make Prayer a Practice in Honesty

We need to look at our fear areas, so we can discover that there is nothing to fear. We need to go to the trouble spot and not attempt to hide from it, and as we explore our being, honestly, we can be set free to choose anew—to become anew. God is not isolated from man. We isolate ourselves by our fears, guilts and hates. As we harbor these, we feel them; we feel the way a problem looks.

The truth will make us free. We begin to go wrong at the point where we deny, pretend or lie to ourselves. Prayer works only to the extent that each is honest with himself and, hence, honest with God.

We have a great capacity to hide from ourselves. Let me illustrate this with a true story: Recently I talked with a woman who was a minister's wife. She had suffered from an ulcerated colon for over ten years. She had through the years lost weight and had, eventually, been forced to give up her teaching career. She was mostly bedridden, and her physician offered her little hope of living. She was living on soup alone. Monthly, her condition worsened. She read a book of mine entitled *Prayer Can Change Your Life*. In this book, she had the opportunity of taking a very simple test that measured two things—hostility and honesty. To her surprise, she discovered that she was extremely hostile. Being a minister's wife, she had maintained that she loved everybody. She had said this for so long that she believed it. Now, suddenly, she was faced with the fact that she harbored deep feelings of resentment. It was impossible to rationalize this away; she had taken the test; she had answered the statements. Apparently, she had suffered long enough. Suffering sometimes brings us to honesty. She turned to the only method she knew—that of prayer. Somehow, now, in this moment of truth, in this moment of revelation, she began to pray to the creative force within herself. She began to enumerate her hatreds, her resentments and verbalized them with feeling. She had every intention of standing in revelation to God and to herself. She poured out everything that she had stored up within herself for years. She then asked for forgiveness and accepted it at once. When she finished with her prayer, she knew that she was healed; she knew she was whole. It wasn't just a wish, a desire; it was a knowing. In this honest dialogue, she had been recreated.

You might say: "But that wasn't positive prayer!" In a way, it was because of its deep honesty. But she didn't stay on the feeling level with the feelings of resentment. She accepted forgiveness, was deeply thankful and, thereafter, was wholly positive. She used healing affirmations and visualizations that kept her moving in a creative direction. Prayer seems to work only to the extent that each is honest with himself and God. Unless we are honest in prayer, we may merely reinforce the escape mechanisms that keep us from wholeness.

Make Prayer a Regular Activity

Learning how to pray and meditate effectively is a skill, and skills are not mastered by a "hit or miss" method. Prayer needs to be a regular activity, a regulative part of our lives. And, as in all therapeusis, there is a follow through—a gradual unfolding.

Regular praying is a re-direction of creativity. It enables us to recognize our creative potential. However, regular praying may not be enough. Many of our modern illnesses arise from our disturbed mental states. Most of the functional disorders, such as duodenal ulcers, ulcerated colon, asthma, stuttering, rheumatoid arthritis, heart trouble and so forth, have as their source of origin fear, guilt and misguided love (hate). Lack of love or misguided love is surely the most important of the three. The goal of all therapy is to awaken or help the person to *express a greater capacity to love and be loved.*

We should pray the last thing at night before we retire, letting our minds be filled with positive, loving thoughts—affirming and giving thanks. Pray, also, the first thing in the morning, setting a happy, positive attitude for the day. Throughout the day, utter positive affirmations, for example: "God, I thank Thee."

Realize there is unlimited power in the words, *I am.* Use your *I am*'s upward for health, wisdom, success and wholeness: *"I am* life"; *"I am* whole"; *"I am* confident"; "God is, and *I am*." With positive, creative emphasis we come to love. Through love we are united with others, with all of life. We feel an identity *with* God, and, yet, we preserve our own individuality.

Possibly the greatest thing about prayer is that it treats the whole person. This is in keeping with the modern thrust of synthesis rather than analysis. With synthesis comes a greater integration, a greater capacity to love. With love comes the feeling that we are one with *All*, yet, we remain ourselves. With this feeling of oneness, we are lifted into the supra-conscious, which is our spiritual center. It is at this level that we receive inspiration and illumination.

One of our great tasks in life is to discover the rest of ourselves . . . to find our place in the thread that weaves through all life. Prayer and meditation is our royal road to this discovery . . . to wholeness. On this road, we are always leading on to new discovery. Philip Wheelwright in his book, *The Burning Fountain,* says: "Man lives always on the verge, always on the borderland of a something more. . . . Indeed, the intimating of a something more, a beyond the horizon, belongs to the very nature of consciousness. . . . To be conscious is not just to be, it is to mean, to intend, to point beyond oneself, to testify that some kind of beyond exists, and to be even on the verge of entering into it."

Finally, prayer links us to the unseen. Prayer can make us whole, so that our electromagnetic being vibrates harmoniously. We can re-program through prayer, so that we identify with creation, with God, with ourselves and others. Prayer lifts us into a new realm, above the mundane, into the spiritual. It moves us beyond doing so we emerge into being.

Through great prayer and meditation, we can realize and accept our divineness and project it out to our world. By this act, we are lifted up and inspire others whose lives we touch. We go from inferiority to self-acceptance, from fear to faith, from guilt to grace and from hate to love; harmony lives in our system.

Effective prayer leads to love. Proper love of ourselves, others and the whole world. At this level, we embrace all mankind. Our world is no bigger than what our heart can embrace; our soul no greater than our capacity and willingness to love. This is the final goal of prayer and meditation—to love. Love outlasts everything.

APERCU OF PRAYER

Mrs. Ena Twigg

A very beautiful "aperçu"—insight on prayer—
came to us from Mrs. Hilary Bray on the Other
Side, through Mrs. Ena Twigg.

And I said, "Show me what I have to learn."

And my teacher said, "Let me show you people praying."

And it was as though I was looking down on many,
many people who were praying. And he said, "That one
is a mother praying for her child. But she is not praying
that God will restore him to health if it is God's will.
She is telling God to make him well. And God is perfect
law, so if it is not in the scheme, the child cannot recov-
er. That prayer does not reach very far. Although it is
intense, and it is pure, it is conditional."

Then I saw a man dressed in a sack, and he was
praying, and he said, "God, I am an unworthy part of
you. But if I can be used, use me."

And the man in the sack had a great light come
down, and it caught his prayer—and my teacher said,
"That prayer has been accepted."

And then we saw a mass of people in uniform, and
they were devising weapons of destruction; and they

were praying that their weapons would be used successfully—and darkness came over. And my teacher said, "Those prayers are not accepted, only by the dark forces. They have no validity and don't reach out."

And we went round and round, and we were looking at an old lady praying for her husband who was dying, and she was saying. "He belongs to You, God, and although I love him dearly, I give him to You."

That prayer reached out. And again a great blaze of light came down. And my teacher said to me—I was weeping—and he said, "Have you learned anything?"

And I said, "Oh, how much I have learned by looking at this thing, much more than I ever learned from my own prayers."

DIMENSIONS OF DEFENSIVE PRAYER

T. N. Tiemeyer

In this selection, Dr. T. N. Tiemeyer discusses
how simple and sincere prayer can be used to
counter the effect of discarnate evil forces.

Reverend Tiemeyer has a B.A. in Social Sciences
from Elmhurst College, and a B. D. Divinity Degree from Eden Theological Seminary. He has
studied at the University of Cincinnati, Chicago
Theological Seminary, Yale University, and the
University of Heidelberg. He is a founder and five-
year chairman of the South Florida Chapter of
Laubach Literacy Movement, and a member of
the Board of Directors of the Survival Research
Foundation. He is presently the pastor of the
Christ Congregation Church in Miami, Florida.

If you accept survival of the human personality, whether by faith or fact, you have probably asked some of
these questions: What happens to the unenlightened or
the atheist? What about the morally ignorant or spiritually degenerate? Do they ever try to return to influence those still living on this plane?

It is illogical to assume that death is a magic wand
which transforms ordinary, worldly-minded people into
perfected divine beings. Passing through the "valley of
the shadow" merely means leaving behind the physical

vehicle. To each is offered the opportunity to transfer
earth consciousness to the infinite and eternal awareness. But suppose the entity rejects this privilege?

People come in many varieties. Some are ignorant,
some evil, some overly sensual, and some corroded with
hatred. Since these are mental attitudes, they survive
death and continue to dominate discarnate beings. Unable or unwilling to accept survival of mind or reality of
spirit, they cannot move on to higher levels. Remaining
as close to the material plane as possible, they may seek
vicarious fulfillment, revenge, or sadistic satisfactions
through those still on the earth plane.

Thus we have a logical basis for belief in spirit possession. In Biblical days this was assumed to be fact. In
the early scientific era such hypotheses were discarded
as medieval superstition. Today, the possibility is again
being seriously considered. Not only is it imperative
that such afflictions be explored, but the preventions
and cures must also be perfected. In this area prayer
has proven itself to be the most powerful defense and
the most potent corrective.

"Deliver us from evil" prayed the Man of Nazareth.
His interpreter, Paul of Tarsus, amplifies the significance of this petition in these words:

"We are not contending against flesh and blood, but
against principalities, against powers, against the world
rulers of this present darkness, against spiritual hosts of
wickedness in the heavenly places. Therefore take the
whole armor of God, that you may be able to withstand
the evil . . . and pray at all times in the Spirit with all
prayers and supplications. To that end keep alert with
all perseverance, making supplication for all the saints"
(Eph. 6:10–18).

When Jesus spoke of the fate of the wicked, let it be
realized that the imagery of Gehenna (translated as

"hell of fire") was not the only one used. Often he spoke of a fate subsequent to this life as being "cast into the outer darkness where there shall be weeping and wailing and gnashing of teeth." How accurately this describes the bewildered souls, released from the flesh, who are not prepared to grasp the significance of a spiritual journey upward! John Bunyan in *Pilgrim's Progress* dramatizes these confused discarnates, praying for them and in his own defense. Albrecht Dürer painted them vividly on his canvases as denizens of hell and offers the protective power in his "Praying Hands."

When Jesus cured the madman of Gadarea he addressed himself to an alien spirit which he identified by name (Mark 5:1–14). His "prayer in the spirit" took the form of a command which expelled the foreign entity. At another time he chided his disciples for their inability to set a possessed person free and revealed this secret formula: "This kind can never be driven out by anything but true prayer and fasting" (Matt. 17:21).

Split personality problems have received much attention from psychologists. Many historical incidents have been carefully researched and documented but few conclusions have been reached. There was the familiar Beauchamp case as recorded by Professor Morton Prince of Tufts College. A true and better known story was that which appeared in the movies under the title *The Three Faces of Eve*. This received more and later attention when a fourth personality made itself evident in the same woman. The strange case of Lurency Vennum of Watseka, Illinois, attracted national interest when for fourteen weeks she assumed the identity of Mary Roff, an entirely different personality who had died some months earlier.

Hugh Lynn Cayce in *Venture Inward* states, "All mental derangement need not and should not be con-

nected with interference or possession by discarnate entities. It might be well, however, to consider the idea
that the psychotic person is one who is aware of activities of the unconscious mind not recognizable to the
average person." Cayce carefully avoids fully commit-
ting himself on this subject. Yet his more illustrious father, Edgar Cayce, offers one of the best examples of an
individual who, while in trance, seemed to be taken
over by a completely different intelligence. There are
also many qualified authorities of mental paranormali-
ties who believe that most cases reported as evidence of
reincarnation can be better explained by temporary
spirit possession.

Sigmund Freud's teacher, Dr. Pierre Janet, recorded
this experience in *Body, Mind and Spirit:* "The patient
uttered words which seemed to be not his own but those
of a possessing spirit and flung about his limbs in obe-
dience to the commands of the demon. I could not cure
the sufferer until I parleyed with the obsessing agent
and, after a long argument, succeeded in compelling
him to obey my orders."

Here is a definite use of a type of prayer to bring
mental healing. Invoking the aid of invisible entities and
sending commands to the discarnate beings is, by broad
definition, a form of prayer. In *Body, Mind and Spirit*
Dr. Elwood Worcester of Boston recorded an even
more complex healing when he dealt with a woman who
was possessed with the spirit of a deceased drug addict.
With the assistance of a woman sensitive, the doctor
pleaded with the possessed woman's deceased family
doctor to lend aid. He, in turn, undertook to expel the
spirit and the woman was free.

Two of my own experiences with possible spirit possession occurred in women gifted with the power of automatic writing. In the Indiana case, the young woman

in her early twenties had been so closely attached to her father that she spurned a normal social life and friends of her own age. When he died suddenly, she was unable to make an adequate adjustment. One day while writing a letter, a force took over her hand and identified himself as her father, bringing greetings, love and kind wishes. Each day she looked forward to these messages which were warm and paternal. One day, however, the tone and penmanship changed. The messages became accusing, then sarcastic, and ultimately obscene. She was powerless to stop the writing. Her family put her into the hands of a psychiatrist.

The second case found me much better prepared to deal with such a situation. The woman this time was more mature and affiliated with my church. She found the messages entertaining until, one day, there was a distinct change in tone. The unknown author warned her to stay away from church, to take instructions only from him in the future, and to ignore the preachings of her pastor. After some months of apprehension, she came to me with the whole story. In the quiet of my study we offered a prayer, surrounding her with angelic forces and requested that no entity make itself manifest that was not in harmony with the Christ mind.

After a bit of indecisiveness, a distinct message was written through her to this effect: "We have removed the evil force which had been trying to dominate you. You were right in using the precautions you did. Never again attempt automatic writing without protecting yourself with prayer. Better still, give it up unless you feel a very strong compulsion."

Susy Smith, prominent author of numerous volumes relating to mental powers and psychic abilities, for more than ten years was under the influence of an intelligence which expressed itself through her automatic typing.

First identifying himself as James, he later claimed to be the late psychologist, William James; then through her fingers he not only wrote an entire book but also re-wrote and revised it no less than four times. A good deal of this manuscript is included in her volumes, *Confessions of a Psychic* and *Evidence of Survival*. Not included in the published works is a chapter on spirit possession; excerpts from that chapter follows:

If you live for yourself alone, considering your pleasures more important than anything else, you will probably die with nothing better on your mind. You will then be an earth-bound spirit. Such an unenlightened individual hangs closely around the earth for many years. If this entity is an alcoholic, he will remain close to a hard drinker, inciting him to further drink so that he can enjoy the experience vicariously. If he took heroin on earth, he still thinks of himself as a user and will live with addicts, urging them on so he can possess or obsess them when they are under drug influence.

Negative thoughts from the earthbound can intrude themselves upon one who is worried or unhappy and make him twice as miserable. Many entities of a more malicious character know they are dead but do not know what to do about it. They continue to hang around the earth, reveling in the kind of life they used to enjoy. Sex is one of their favorite subjects as you can well imagine. The best way to keep such as these from you is to be the clean living, positive thinking type who does not interest them in the least.

If you are weak-willed and negative in your personality, they may pressure you to indulge excessively in your weaknesses, commit crimes, or even

drive you to suicide. Realize that you can protect
yourself. Insist orally that you will not allow anyone to influence you who does not come from God
in love and peace. Affirm this often, and believe it.

The stark reality of the evil spirit menace has been
experienced by Ingrid Sherman, who for two years as-
sisted Tony Agpaoa in performing psychic surgery in
the Philippines. "There is a strange magnetism in those
islands," she states, "which is conducive to greater activity of sinister psychic elements. I have frequently
been under attack by black forces and once I was
dragged around my room at night by an invisible entity.
At another time I was visited by what sounded like a
300-pound monster bounding across the living room,
coming into my bedroom, and hovering over my bed,
breathing heavily."

When asked how she protected herself, she replied,
"In this last incident I screamed for St. Theresa. I then
saw a vision of her statue and heard her voice assuring
me that everything would be all right." She has used
various other modes of protection including a projected
white light which she forms into a sword and uses to
fight the intruders. Most frequently, however, her means
of defense has been a simple, informal prayer. "My saving grace," she states, "was in the confidence I had built
up over the years while going along the road of believing in God's forces. Cultivate the awareness that God is
there and that your spirit guides are backing you. Then
just call on God in prayer and you will receive all the
help you need."

The efficacy of prayer in expelling troublesome
spirits has long been recognized by the Christian church
which has provided standard prayers for this purpose.
Jewish rituals also provide the rabbi with such prayers

to expel the "dibbuch" or evil spirit. Various forms of exorcism have had ecclesiastical approval although no one standard ceremony seems to be adequate for all occasions.

Benevolent assistance has been invoked in various but effective ways through the annals of history. Elisha in the Old Testament found it possible to call upon such a powerful host of defenders that his servant, when given clairvoyance, described the protectors as an army of fiery chariots (2 Kings 6:15,16). The prayers of Shadrach, Meshach, and Abednego brought them a fourth person to protect them in the fiery furnace (Dan. 4:25). The prayer disciplines of Jesus created such a powerful insulation against evil that when his enemies sought to cast him from the hilltop, they found they could not hold on to him (Luke 4:29,30). When the temple soldiers came to arrest him, they were unable to lay hands upon him until he, figuratively speaking, turned off the power (John 18:4–6).

Strange assortments of techniques have been employed by those seeking protection from "the forces of darkness." These include singing of hymns, calling aloud sacred words with expectations of magic results, uttering mystical vowel sounds, making the sign of the cross, encasing one's self symbolically within a wall of spirit fire, etc. People have put their faith in a variety of equipment to make themselves "invulnerable," such as rosaries, pentagrams, special gems, holy water, protective light rays, musical vibrations, crucifixes, wolfbane, incense, ointments, dogwood or mandrake root. None of these by themselves has ever been proven as effective as simple and sincere prayer.

If one admits the possibility of earthbound spirits trying to possess or obsess the carnate individual, one must realize that it cannot happen if that person is fully in control of his consciousness and will. However, there are many people whose wills are weak and whose minds are open to penetration. These include the alcoholic, the drug addict, the sexually promiscuous, compulsive gamblers, enslaved cigarette smokers, and those who are unable to control excessive eating habits. Any weakness in will power leaves an opening into which the discarnate evil forces may enter to express themselves or take temporary control.

The danger of leaving the door open is not only for those who have addictions and bad habits. There are many times in the life of the average self-controlled individual when his mind is open to assault. In sickness or extreme fatigue, the self is vulnerable. Under anaesthetic in surgery or even in a dentist's chair, evil forces are believed to have entered. The most common time of danger is in sleep. No wonder we are told that the fifteen minutes before sleep is called the day's most critical quarter hour. Who knows what degenerative elements may attempt to slip into your mind while your consciousness is out of the control room? All the more reason why prayer is so essential before sleeping!

One can now understand the value of teaching children simple bedtime prayers. A highly effective one is that which Hansel and Gretel sing in Humperdinck's opera, with these words, "When at night I go to sleep, fourteen angels watch do keep" etc. I know adults who invoke the four guardian angels, Raphael, Michael, Gabriel, and Uriel to watch over them from the four directions. Each individual is challenged to devise his own prayer protection so that his sleep will be guarded, untroubled, and safe from invasion by infernal entities.

Lew Smith, a converted Jew, has devised a unique way which to his satisfaction reveals the number of undesirable entities in any person at a given time. Once ascertained, he uses a simple prayer to expel the negative influence. I write from first-hand experience when I state that this is even effective when given over the phone. Skeptic though I was, I cannot deny that I felt a definite tingling, starting in the central pelvic portions and moving in both directions to head and feet, followed by a feeling of exhilaration. I make no effort to explain, only to record this unusual reaction to a prayer designed to cleanse one from the influence of harmful or unhealthy spirit forces.

For those who want to try it or who feel the need of such spiritual therapy, here is this prayer, both time-tested and personally attested to:

"Dear God, cleanse, clear, fill, and encapsulate me in the white Christ light of healing and protection. Remove all negative energies and entities from me and send them to their proper plane. Then close my aura against their return and in their place put the highest and most powerful vibrations. Thank you, Father."

PRAYER: HOW AND WHY IN THE LIGHT OF BUDDHISM

Princess Poon Pismai Diskul

Princess Poon Pismai Diskul examines, within the context of Buddhism, the question of how and why one prays. Her exploration of the techniques of and reasons for prayer shows how with sincerity, sacrifice, and selflessness one can stay on the Right Path.

The Princess first became widely known for her early work on Buddhism, *Sasanaguna* ("The Value of Religion"). Now in her seventies, she has long been a leading participant in Buddhist activities. Her devotion to the cause of world peace and her painstaking efforts as president of the World Fellowship of Buddhists are acknowledged by all who know her. The Princess received the Royal Medal of the Most Illustrious Order of Chula Chom Klao from the King for her humanitarian service in the cause of Buddhism, and she was the first woman president of the Buddhist Association of Thailand.

The role of prayer in Buddhism is both simple and complicated, both easy and difficult to understand, depending partly on the angle of approach and partly on the person who approaches it.

To the question "How to Pray and Why?" we must first ask, "By what is prayer meant in Buddhism?"

To put it in a nutshell, prayer in Buddhism means the desire repeatedly expressed to remind oneself of one's spiritual goal so that one will not waver in the presence of adverse forces of temptations and threats and so that the wish expressed may be achieved through one's own development and maturity as a result of one's own efforts.

To elaborate, Buddhism has as its essential doctrine the Law of Karma determining that, in the Buddha's own words, "Self is the refuge of self," "Be your own refuge," "You must make your own efforts," "Purity and blemish are individual affairs," and several others.

Obviously to some the above quotations may seem to be discouraging and depressing, for it appears that everybody has to struggle alone unaided, relying solely on self-help and being unable to expect assistance from anybody in any way at any time. Should this be absolutely true, then even the Buddha would have no place at all and Buddhism would not benefit mankind in any way whatever.

Scripturally speaking, the place of the Buddha can be seen in his own words: "I am the pointer of the Way."

Now "pointer of the Way" has several shades or depths of meaning, depending upon the levels of development or maturity of the person who "treads the Way thus pointed."

You may picture the Buddha as a person who stands by the wayside, pointing to the travelers at some remote point far away and telling them to go on, not to sidestep from the main Path—and you will not be wrong, although such a picture is far from perfect and may cause a serious misunderstanding to many.

To get a better idea of this, just study the life of the Buddha. You can see how the Buddha and, of course, his Noble Disciples, underwent constant and complex

troubles through their indefatigable efforts to "point the
Way" to those who had not known the right Way and
also to those who knew the right Way but preferred to
sidestep from or to stop on the Way. To cite only a
few examples: the training and conversion of the Five
Ascetics; of the 1,000 fire-hermits; of Nanda, his half-
brother; of Bhikkhu Tissa, whose whole body was covered with running sores (the Buddha helped clean those
sores himself); and the Finger-Necklace Robber will
give us a better picture of how arduous and exacting
was the task of "pointing the Way."

Except in the case of some disciples (such as Bahiya
and Sankicca Samanera) who won through to attainment rapidly and with ease, in most cases to "point the
Way" was *never* to stand passively by the wayside,
pointing to an obscure place on the horizon. Even in the
case of the seemingly easy attainment the task was
"more than what meets the eye." It was not merely
talking or cramming the facts into the listeners' heads
but it necessitated the Buddha's prior attainment in
order to know what level of attainment the listener had
come up to at the moment. This required the power of
clairvoyance and telepathy before the Teacher could
"point the Way" further again so the listener could see a
little further ahead. This process could go on steadily to
the end *provided, of course, that the person in question
matured enough spiritually to be led on to the end.*

If the person was unable to go on, the Buddha would
stop for the time being, to go on again soon. The best
example of this may be seen in the case of the Buddha's
first sermon. At the end of this sermon, the Buddha recognized that the Venerable Kon Danna had realized a
great part of his teaching and had crossed the Rubicon
of worldlings, but he stopped there and continued his
sermon on the days that followed. These examples serve

to show how "pointing the Way" is by no means as easy a task as the words imply. In absolute terms, it is a two-way affair, depending upon the Karma of each individual (that is, how mature he or she is), upon how far or how fast he or she can be informed of the various sign-posts on the Way, and partly upon the ability of the person who undertakes to "point the Way."

Bhikkhus in various lands are supposed to say their prayers every day when they chant in the morning and/or in the evening. In Thailand there are, for instance, the passages which say, "This devoted reverence having been paid to the Triple Gem, through whatever merit gained thereof, let not misfortune come to pass," and "To the Buddha I surrender this body-and-mind . . . by the power of uttering this truthfulness may I prosper in the doctrine of the Buddha." These and others serve as verbal reminders of the prior resolutions and also as expressions of the inner goal. Buddhists understand that they are required also to act accordingly: sincerely, sacrificially, and selflessly. Above all, we Buddhists know we can be helped in proportion to our own self-help (that is, through our own Karma). The more we try to help ourselves, the more we can be helped—by our own Karma, which enables us to draw on help from the sources where help can be drawn. This, therefore, is the technique of *how to pray,* in the light of Buddhism.

As regards the question *why to pray,* let us consider first some incidents happening to all of us in our every-day life. When we are ill, for example, we need the doctor's help in the form of advice and medicine, for as laymen we are unable to help ourselves. But then we are required to follow the doctor's advice and take the medicine ourselves. None can do this for us. Again, in education we need our teachers' help in doing our exercises and homework, but we must help ourselves in time of examination. None can help us in such times. In these cases *we are helped in order that we may be able to help ourselves.*

Now we come to the answer *why.* Buddhists "pray" to the Triple Gem (remind themselves verbally or mentally) because they want to strengthen their will power after they have studied his teaching and known intellectually what is right and what is wrong. They know that to "pray" in the spirit mentioned above is self-strengthening and self-encouraging so that, when occasion arises, they can fight the battle of their lives alone, being at that moment strengthened and encouraged by their previously accumulated Karma in the form of sincerity, sacrifice, and selflessness. The more they are sincere, sacrificial, and selfless, the better they can fight against temptations and threats and the sooner their wishes will be granted and their prayers "answered."

Thus in Buddhism a person's Karma, or spiritual maturity, is the sum of all possibilities. We can have or be anything if we care and dare to pay the price—a price not of gold and silver but of the steady and progressive accumulation of good Karma through walking the Right Path pointed out to us again and again with every step of our progress on that Path. To do so we must remember and survey our purposes as often as possible, and repeated "prayer" with the attitude mentioned above is a key to success.

However, frankly speaking, I am of the opinion that the spirit of prayer that characterizes Buddhism can be found to underlie all religious doctrines that are worth the name, the difference being the degree of emphasis and obviousness and also the way of expression. For whereas Buddhism speaks out definitely and unequivocally, in other doctrines the spirit of prayer is sometimes obscured by legends and poetic or figurative expressions and at other times is left understood and needs to be read between the lines, so to speak. There might be various reasons, due to circumstances and the background of listeners at a particular time, and the masters of various religious doctrines are not to blame for this.

To sum up, it is clear that in a relative world we cannot always depend on others' help; nor can we completely boast our self-help. Having been helped by our Master's injunctions, be he the Buddha, Christ, or Mohammed, we must make our own efforts so that we can be better helped and so that we can attain a condition where we shall no longer depend on anybody's help.

And the best way to keep us on the Right Path is to observe, warn, and remind ourselves so that we shall not forget or be led astray on the Way. Repeated prayer, whether mental or verbal, *with the attitude of mind and the mode of practice earlier mentioned,* is the technique for this purpose. This is the answer to *how to pray* in the light of Buddhism.

Now, everybody has a weak point. Repeated prayer, in the sense and method above-mentioned, can help build up for him an immunizing power against attacks and setbacks. In "prayer" a Buddhist builds up a Karma, or cause, that will produce a Vipaka, or effect, he wishes for. It is a self-strengthening and self-encouraging process. It is, in other words, a case of *"Deserve* before you *desire."*

PRAYER FOR PEACE AND HAPPINESS

Ahmad Kuftaro, Grand Mufti of Syria

Sheikh Ahmad Kuftaro urges that we return to faith and worship to bring about the brotherhood of man that will unite nations and bring peace to humanity.

His Excellency the Grand Mufti of Syria received his Ph.D. in the field of Islamic preaching. He is a world lecturer on Islam, comparative religions, Muslim-Christian cooperation, and cooperation among heavenly religions. He is also head of AL-ANSAR—Social, Cultural and Religious Society in Syria, head of the Supreme Council of Fatwa, Grand Mufti of Syria, permanent member of the World Islamic Organizations and Conferences, and member of the People Council.

Science says our earth was a burning gas which cooled and froze and became a planet carrying living things after the inoculated seed turned into a perfect human being. It also says that our galaxy, together with millions of others, consists of tremendous worlds, some of which are probably inhabited. The human mind is unable to count them nor know their dimensions or boundaries or what they do contain. Myriad laws govern them and keep them in their courses. It is astonishing to look at the minute cells of the brain, liver, blood or others and see how they perform their function with great efficiency and according to laws away from which they cannot divert. There we witness creation and discipline. But when we cast an overall look at the unity of the universe and its laws, from its galaxies to its cells and atoms with their perfect harmony and creative consistency which have no fault or disorder, surely we will admit that this universe has a great Maker who is All Knowing, Merciful and Wise. He granted man his existence and life. He supported him with powers and means by which he attained his aspirations and achieved his goals.

When man contemplates his existence on his earthly planet which is smaller than the smallest atom of sand in the biggest desert when compared with the galaxies and the infinite worlds, how small he will find himself and how much his poor being is in need of a helpful great Creator! He is in need of His kindness especially when he is in the midst of distress wherein his means of rescue and deliverance have run short. I think under these circumstances man has to look for a means by which he can accomplish a true communion with the great Creator who is the source of power and boundless compassion and by which he can entreat His care and beg for His mercy. This true communion can grant him a well of divine wisdom and true inspiration which can guide him on the right path and give him spiritual happiness and success in all ways of life.

God is aware of the defects of man and his countless needs, so He had granted him what he lacked before he asked for what he wanted. God had opened the gate of response before man asked Him. He says in the Koran: "Pray unto me and I will hear your prayer" (XL, 60).

The most wonderful bounty He ever gave us is the system of prayer which is a school whose instructors are the prophets and their disciples. They have taught us how to utilize this great means with proper efficiency. They have instructed us at the school of prayer with true angelic education whose graduates are adorned with perfect humanity and the most virtuous conduct.

By means of prayer we can prescribe remedy for our spiritual weaknesses and nourishment for our souls. It can give us the power to conquer the spirit of evil and sin which destroys man's happiness in his inner soul, his society and his world. This spiritual power enabled the prophets and their followers to accomplish full success in achieving their aspirations and ridding themselves of their crises. Prayer was the fortress in which they took refuge in extremities. They could, by prayer, bring up the virtuous, perfect, and happy man.

If I were to mention in this short work what blessings and fruit I and my friends and my faithful disciples have got through prayer, it would take pages and pages. With God's various kinds of help impossible wishes have been granted and hard difficulties have been surmounted. Fear and trouble have been changed into tranquillity and security, disease into sound health, perplexity and hesitation in making great decisions into infallible inspiration and successful thought.

How to Pray

When the worshipper says his prayers, he has to be clean both in body and apparel with the scent of perfume spreading from him. He has to stand before God in regret for his sins and bad deeds, with a determination to get rid of them, even change them into virtues and good deeds. He has to decide from all his heart to be straightforward and follow the path of good and

avoid the path of evil. He has to turn with all his intellect and senses to his Lord the Creator, fearing His
greatness and imploring Him to pardon his sins and
vices with full confidence of His bounty and mercy and
confidence that his prayers will surely be accepted.
Thus, obstacles and barriers between the worshipper
and God vanish and man's spiritual communion with
his Lord is achieved. His happiness with its rapture di-
minishes all sensual pleasures and makes it easy for him
to bear all shocks and misfortunes. God says in the
Koran: "O ye who believe! Seek help in steadfastness
and prayer. Lo! Allah is with the steadfast" (II, 153).

Saying prayer under the guidance of efficient instructors is the vitamins and lively nourishment to the spirit
of man. This sacred communion infuses the spirit of the
worshipper with the attributes of God: with mercy,
love, sympathy, kindness, and generosity for the good
of man. All moral virtues towards the near and the far
and towards all creatures become his. Prophet Mohammed says: "All creatures are God's dependents; the
most favored by God is he who is most helpful to
them." These virtues do not only accomplish peace for
man in this world but also cooperation and brotherhood, bliss and tranquillity, happiness, rest of conscience, and satisfaction. Moreover, in the soul of the
worshipper some divine traits will appear, as in a drop
of ocean water there exist all its properties. These traits
are reflected in his heart as a reflection appears in the
clear mirror. Thus man's power is derived from God's
power and his wisdom from His wisdom, and his forbearance from His forbearance. The forces of nature
are at his command thanks to this lively true prayer. I
do not exaggerate if I say that due to this communion
between man and his Lord and with the effects and
blessings of prayer Abraham, Moses, Jesus Christ and

Mohammed, peace be upon them, could heal the ill and could foresee the unseen and foretell the future. With this prayer their wishes were granted and they could perform miracles. The spiritual powers of the worshipper develop so much that his sixth sense becomes alive, enabling him to hear and see what the ordinary eye and ear are unable to see and hear. God's angels and spirit will teach and guide him by means of divine inspiration along the path of good and righteousness in all his bodily and spiritual affairs in the same manner as the prophets and the faithful believers before them had been taught.

If the man of today is far away from faith and worship, it is not because his human nature is corrupted or he is no longer apt to accept them. It is because faith and worship have lost much of their beauty and vitality which used to attract all kinds of men in the past. The mere chanting of the holy books and the mere contentment with the bodily movements in prayer will yield no fruit of virtue in the human character. To say prayers with a sinful spirit will not enable the worshipper to accomplish his spiritual and materialistic objectives and aspirations. This dead worship will not revive the spirit nor achieve any communion with the spirit of God. This communion will surely call for God's help and care for the worshipper and God's response to his wishes. Worship will not attain its goals nor give its fruit if it is not on the level God enjoins and the manner prophets and messengers taught the believers. If we examine the system of true worship preached by prophets and messengers, we realize why man in the past cherished it whereas the present-day man has neglected it. Christ says: "In your prayer do not be careful of verbosity, for God looks only into the heart. Many pray but their hearts are full of evil, so they are not serious in what

they say." He also says: "God does not accept the
prayer of a man with a filthy heart: all sea water does
not purgate whoever cherishes sins in his heart." He
also says: "Whoever prays thoughtlessly mocks his
Lord."

Prophet Mohammed says: "Who persistently knocks
at the gate will certainly get it open." The Koran says:
"I answer the prayer of the suppliant when he crieth
unto Me. So let them hear My call and let them trust in
Me, in order that they may be led aright" (II, 186).

Mohammed relates the following as said by God:
"Not all who say their prayers are good worshippers. I
accept the prayers of those who are humble to My
greatness and refrain from forbidden sensual desires,
and do not persist in their disobedience to Me. They
feed the hungry, clothe the needy, have pity on the injured, and give refuge to strangers; they do all that for
My sake. I swear by My glory and majesty, the light of
their faces is brighter than the light of the sun. I vow to
make their ignorance learning and their gloom brilliance. Whenever they ask Me, I readily fulfil their
wishes and provide what they beg Me for. My angels
are their safeguards and they are always in My Providence. They are like Paradise whose fruit never decays
nor changes."

And when we read Matthew: "And all things, whatsoever ye shall ask in prayer, believing, ye shall receive," it is not strange to see the Koran give witness to
Matthew of this truth. It says: "Pray unto me and I will
hear your prayer" (XL, 60).

In the gospel according to Barnabas it shows this aim
more clearly: "If a man says his prayer properly, he
shall surely get what he begs for." Then the Koran
comes at last, to emphasize this truth which all divine
religions have agreed upon. It says: "Prosperous is he

who purifies himself, and remembers the name of his
Lord and prays! Nay! but ye prefer the life of this
world, while the hereafter is better and more lasting.
Verily, this was in the book of yore,—the books of
Abraham and Moses."

By virtue of his knowledge and endeavours, man
managed to discover many sorts of germs which used to
kill millions of human creatures, and consequently he
was able to invent drugs and vaccines which have anni-
hilated most of these germs that used to cause misery to
mankind.

It is high time present-day man realized war and its
devastating effects and catastrophes: orphans, widows
and deformed or distorted warriors on a large scale.
Hasn't man understood yet that wars are the result of
the microbes of greed and avarice, of selfishness and de-
ceit rooted in merciless hearts and brutal souls? We
scarcely perceive any human emotions or moral virtues
in the bodily frame of man at present.

All those vices resulted from lack of genuine worship
and loss of the spirit and essence of religion or faith.
Have the contemporary researchers taken into consider-
ation the necessity of ridding humanity of these fatal
microbes which threaten to destroy civilization to the
same extent as putting an end to the germs of the body?
Will there be endeavours to resort to the drug-stores of
prophets and apostles after brushing them of fanaticism
and dogmatism and supplying them with true thought
and mental freedom? Perhaps we shall restore thereby
the efficiency of the drugs which Abraham, Moses,
Jesus and Mohammed made use of to cure humanity of
its epidemic, spiritual diseases.

Is there any possibility, as a first step, for creating a
Christian-Islamic co-operation for renovating genuine
faith and vivid worship in order to attain love, fraternity

and sympathy? Jesus Christ said, "Love your relations
as yourself." Mohammed said, "None of you is a true
believer unless he loves for his brethren what he loves
for himself." It is impossible to achieve this before improving the neglected worship system which is nowadays inadequate for lack of capable trainers. It is essential, too, to renovate faith in human souls which suffer
from lack of love, fraternity, co-operation and human
sympathy. Human souls are inflicted with dearth of
moral virtues such as truth, faithfulness and honesty.
We have exchanged the blossoms of our souls for the
thorns of atheism and the vices of tyranny and imperial-
ism. Everyone knows that the Big Powers spend countless sums of money on the production of military equipment such as trans-continental rockets and all sorts of
bombs and space ships. Moreover, scientific institutes
and industrial corporations spend huge amounts of
wealth on experimentation and research work for the
sake of improving man's implements. Have the people
in charge ever thought of re-instituting lost humanity
and its dignified virtuous morals by means of Faith and
Worship based on learning and the mind?

It is possible to hold a permanent conference to effect co-operation among the heavenly religions—pri-
marily between Islam and Christianity since there is
much resemblance between them, especially when one
knows that about one-third of the Koran treats of de-
fence and praise of Christ, Moses, their holy books and
of all the prophets in the Bible.

I address all believers and free people throughout the
world who are concerned about peace and humanity,
and urge them to study this proposal of mine for which
I have been striving for the last 25 years all over the
world. I daresay we may, by this experiment (which is
able to bring about mercy, peace and humanitarianism,

and which I dearly cherish), go back to the faith or belief which was applied by Abraham, Moses, Jesus and Mohammed. Let's resort to true worship which is the greatest link between God and us, with our hands full of His bounties and gifts, and as Saint Matthew said: "And all things, whatsoever ye shall ask in prayer, believing, ye shall receive."

CAN MODERN MAN PRAY?

Dr. Robert I. Kahn

Modern man has trouble with prayer. The new
scientific outlook makes it difficult to believe as did
our fathers of yesterday. Rabbi Kahn explores the
subject and responds with a new outlook on an old
practice.

Dr. Robert I. Kahn, Rabbi of Congregation
Emanu El of Houston, Texas was ordained in
1935 by the Hebrew Union College-Jewish Institute of Religion. Presently the President of the
Central Conference of American Rabbis, he was
for six years the Chairman of its Liturgy Committee. He has been visiting lecturer on Homiletics
at his alma mater, on Jewish Mysticism at the
Jung Center, and on Judaism at St. Thomas University. He writes a weekly column in the *Houston
Chronicle*, "Lessons for Life." His more recent
books include *Ten Commandments for Today*, and
The Letter and the Spirit. Rabbi Kahn has been
given honorary awards by the Boy Scouts of
America, the Freedoms Foundation, the Four
Chaplains Chapel, and the Scottish Rite.

Prayer is the natural outreach of the human spirit toward the spirit of the universe, as innate as our response
to music, as natural as our eye for beauty, as much a
part of us as our longing for love.

Nevertheless, as natural as it may be, many of us

moderns have trouble praying. Although unable to rid ourselves of the longing, we have lost our faith in its value. I shall never forget the hospital patient who literally clung to my hand and wept, "Rabbi, I want to pray but I can't. I no longer believe in prayer."

How many of us echo that cry, and how we envy those who are capable of faith-filled worship. There was a woman in my community who had weathered storm after storm with so serene an expression, and so deep a gift of prayer, that everyone used to say, "I wish I had faith like that. I wish I could pray like that."

We have a problem. The hunger for communion is still there, but for many the food has been spoiled. The contemporary thought-patterns of our world have shaken our belief in the efficacy of prayer, and the liturgy of our fathers has lost its meaning for us. Both their ideas and their language seem out of date.

Our Jewish prayer book was born in a far different world than ours. The Biblical psalms, the Talmudic *berachot* (blessings), and the medieval *piyyutim* (prayer-poems) were all written in a different context of thought. God was regarded not only as the Creator of the world, but He was also its daily overseer. He was not only First Cause, but intermediate and immediate cause of all events. The rains fell by His will, the drought followed His command. Hurricanes and calm weather, sickness and health, defeat and victory all were dependent on Him. In such a world, worship was man's avenue of appeal, adoration was a way to God, thanksgiving was due Him, and petitions were freely addressed to the Almighty. Our prayer book is built on this faith in the value and efficacy of prayer.

In our day, God is regarded as far removed from the daily workings of the world. The universe is no longer a stage upon which He raises and lowers curtains or produces sound effects. In our contemporary world-view, the universe is a machine, wonderfully and fearfully made, and (most agree) the work of a Creative Intelligence, but still a machine, ALL of whose workings can be explored by scientific means, and described by so-called laws of nature. Its linked and interlinked chains of chemical and physical cause and effect are quite impersonal. To imagine that prayer can effectuate any change in the workings of this machine would be to indulge in wishful thinking. "For what would we thank God?" the scientific mind asks. "The law of gravity? And for what petition Him? The third principle of thermodynamics?"

More than this, the Creator of this world, once regarded as a near and familiar figure, whose central concern was this earth and the inhabitants thereof, who spoke in thunder to Moses and in a still small voice to Elijah, is now revealed to be the Deity of a world so vast that the mind boggles at its infinities. The earth, in Bible days the center of the universe, is now seen as a tiny planet circling a piddling star which is fifteen thousand light years from the center of its Milky Way galaxy, which in turn is but one of many galaxies, all of them two million and more light years away. "When I behold the heavens, O Lord, what is man?" How can a God who has flung out the stars across the infinite space years attend the prayer of a puny human being who lies weeping on a lonely sickbed?

But our spirits are still hungry, and so there are many who have revised their conception of prayer. No longer able to believe it to be a dialogue between man and God, they take it to be a soliloquy between man and his "better self." No longer convinced of its *objective* efficacy, they praise its *subjective* usefulness as an outlet for the heart's longings.

Let us suppose for a moment that this were so, that prayer were nothing but a cry shouted into an unanswering void. Would this negate its value or its power? Not entirely. Even subjective prayer can be, has been, enormously effective, changing the objective world by its change of subjective persons in that world. The focussing of attention which worship can achieve, and the explosive energies which meditation can mobilize introduce new links into the chain of cause and effect. The chemical and the physical do respond to the spiritual.

Even if one assumes that what Moses experienced at the burning bush was only a mirage, still, what happened later in Egypt was a fact, and the memory of it a powerful force in history. And even if the Maccabees were only talking to themselves, they talked themselves into preserving Judaism. Yes, even were worship only a subjective experience, prayer would be powerful in restoring personal health, powerful in achieving social reform, powerful in the re-writing of history.

But it is my conviction that prayer is more than a subjective experience, more than a soliloquy. Even as a sunflower on a cloudy day turns toward a sun that is hidden, so the human spirit reaches out to a spirit that is there. And this conviction does not require a leap of faith, nor a closing of the eyes to all the accumulation of scientific research and saying, "Nevertheless, I believe!" On the contrary, science itself, in recent groping experiments and hesitant hypotheses on the growing edge of research in psychology, in medicine, in biology, stands on the threshold of the re-discovery of the spiritual aspects of the universe.

Space does not permit the detailing of all the evidence. Let me simply refer you to men and to books and their conclusions.

Carl Jung: "Anyone who has the least knowledge of

the parapsychological materials which already exists and has been thoroughly verified, will know that so-called telepathic phenomena are undeniable facts."

Psychosomatic medicine has introduced a new view-point in the medical profession. Medical researchers who once conceived of the body as a chemico-physical machine have come to realize that there are non-mechanical factors at work. Where once the minister was regarded by some doctors as an intruder in the sick-room, the hospital Chaplain is now a member of the healing team. "Heal us, O Lord, and we shall be healed."

Dr. Edmund Sinnott, Professor of Botany at Yale University, has put a lifetime of study and research into the physical and chemical processes of plant growth. In his book, *The Biology of the Spirit,* he describes a series of biological findings which reveal purposeful goal-seeking "spiritual" qualities in the natural proc-esses. "This self-regulating, pattern-seeking quality of all life may be *described* in chemical terms, but it cannot be explained nor understood except in spiritual terms."

Pierre Teilhard de Chardin, paleontologist, in *The Phenomenon of Man* unfolds a thesis which is based upon the law of conservation of energy. By this law, everything now in existence was always there. Evolution is the progressive unfolding of qualities that were all previously present, but in so "thin" a form, so to speak, as not to be evident. Before man, there was no self-conscious spiritual groping, yet that quality of man was embryonic in the universe. In sum, that same spiritual quality which was present in the chaos of whirling nebulae, and is found by Sinnott in the groping purpose-fulness of plant life, comes to flower in the soul of man.

I would also recommend the reading of Loren Eise-ley's *The Unexpected Universe.* This naturalist, student and biographer of Charles Darwin, lifts the heart and feeds the spirit. For real inspiration, read the chapter entitled "The Star Thrower."

So it is with the sociologist Peter L. Berger in his book, *A Rumor of Angels,* which is subtitled "Modern Society and the Rediscovery of the Supernatural." He turns for "rumors of angels" not to philosophy, nor to science, but to the structure of man's heart, his love of order, his capacity for play, his faith in the future. It is a stimulating book, and will open windows in your soul.

All of these contemporary witnesses testify that we are formed by the same forces, chemical, physical and spiritual, which hold the stars in their orbit, thrust up the mountains, scoop out the seas, bring the rose to bloom, teach the hawk to fly, the horse to neigh. "If I climb up unto the heavens, behold Thou art there, and if I go to the ends of the earth, behold Thou art there."

Prayer is not the lonely cry of a "tailless monkey playing ape to his dreams," nor a shout into an empty void answered only by its own echo. Prayer is the spirit within us reaching out to the Spirit of the universe; and prayer is that Spirit responding to us. Even as the sun, ninety-two million miles away, spinning through space with the planets in its train, still (as Galileo pointed out) ripens a bunch of grapes as though that were all it had to do, so does the God of the infinite light years lean down close to the suffering to hear their cry.

And thus we realize that although the prayers of our fathers may seem naive, they penetrated intuitively to the core of truth—that prayer is dialogue between the spirit of man and the Spirit of God.

Yet, as natural as the hunger for dialogue with God may be, it must still be learned. Just as the eye must be trained to appreciate beauty, and the ear, great music, so the soul must be taught to pray.

How shall we learn to pray?

Luckily, we do not have to start from scratch; we can begin by learning how our fathers prayed.

To understand our Jewish liturgy takes study (and this is true I believe of all traditional forms of worship). Our liturgy resembles classical poetry. Anyone who has taken a course in literature knows that without a knowledge of Greek mythology, it is difficult to make sense of much English poetry. But with that knowledge, those poems not only become clear to the mind, but glow with beauty as well. The study of traditional prayer will make the seemingly arbitrary symbols and oddly worded blessings stand out like the colors in a medieval painting that has been cleansed and restored.

Another aspect of our prayer book which we need to understand is the fact that it speaks from and to so many different hearts. People are not alike religiously any more than they are physically. Some like their faith all systematic and intellectual; others like their faith all mystic and emotional. The prayer book was written by men of equally wide differences. The *Adon Olam* expresses the intellectual precision of a Maimonides, the *L'cho Dodi*, the poetic mysticism of Kabbalism. The prayer book speaks to every heart. There are prayers for the quiet of the study, for militant social action, for the sick at heart, for the radiant of faith.

Would you learn to pray? Begin with the book of prayer.

And then continue by making your prayer a *keva*, a fixed habit, in your private devotions, your family rituals and your public worship. Customarily we separate these and weigh their comparative importance. Personally, I cannot see much distinction between them, nor any possibility of getting along without all of them. A private prayer is like an aria sung in the shower, the family ritual is like singing the same selection together around the piano in the living room, public worship is like attending a concert. All enrich, all supplement. In private devotions there is a depth of insight that cannot be measured; in family devotions a quality of warmth beyond description; and among the "multitude keeping holy day," a limitless strengthening and broadening of faith. And all of these must be regular, our private exercises in a daily time and place, our family devotions at the table, daily and on Sabbaths and holy days, our public worship weekly. We pump our exercycles religiously, keep our golf dates ceremoniously, and buy season tickets to the symphony so we won't miss a one. Let us learn to pray by regular prayer.

But the key to prayer, as the Psalmists knew, is the mood of prayer.

Leo Baeck was quoted recently by one of his students as saying that "a person achieves real *Kavanah* [inspired devotion] in rare moments." So our faith supplies us a prayer book which helps us reach "at least a certain height." The prayer book can reach high levels of inspiration, and high levels of inspiration can lift the prayer book above routine.

I would suggest another way to lift the level of the prayer book's impact. The creating and sustaining of a deep mood can best be achieved by recall, a recall of those moments in your life when time stood still, when you felt at one with the universe. It may have been a sunset, or your first glimpse of a snow-capped mountain, or looking at your sleeping baby. There have been moments in all our lives, whether we called them prayerful or not, when awe and wonder rose in our hearts like the tide on the shore, and at such moments we knew, without words, the meaning of life.

Would you make your routine prayers meaningful?

Close your eyes and remember moments of grandeur and glory.

And if there have not yet been such moments, and if your every effort at communion seems dry and sterile, all I can say is keep trying.

Perhaps a personal experience will help clarify what I mean.

In high school, my senior English teacher taught us that Shakespeare was the greatest of dramatists, and *Hamlet* the greatest of dramas. I accepted her judgment but did not appreciate the play at all. The soliloquy was over my head, the madness of Ophelia seemed without motive, the graveyard puns made no impression.

Then, at the University of Cincinnati, where I majored in English, a professor made the same claim. This time I tried to find out why he felt *Hamlet* the greatest of plays. But I could not understand the play, its characters, nor its greatness. And, sophomore-like, I decided the whole thing was a plot; no one had the courage to say the king was really naked.

Twenty years later, I read that Laurence Olivier would play Hamlet, and so I went to see the movie. Nothing! And this time I was angry. The whole world couldn't be all wrong. So on coming home that very night, I took out my Shakespeare and read *Hamlet* until two in the morning. No contact. It was still beyond my ability to see what moved everyone else.

Ten more years later, a performance of *Hamlet* was advertised by a Houston theater-in-the-round. You would think that by this time I would have known better, but I went. And I do not know what happened that night, nor why, but suddenly *Hamlet* came alive. I realized why Ophelia had gone mad, I doubled up in laughter at the gravediggers' puns, I recognized what the soliloquy was about. Now I knew why *Hamlet* was called the greatest of dramas. It had taken years, but I knew, I knew.

And so it will be if our souls reach out in prayer again and again to the soul of the universe. Jeremiah said it best: "If with all your hearts you truly seek Me, you shall find Me."

BIBLIOGRAPHY:

Berger, Peter L. *A Rumor of Angels*, Garden City, N.Y.: Doubleday & Co. Inc.

de Charden, Pierre Teilhard *The Phenomenon of Man*, New York: Harper & Row

Eiseley, Loren *The Unexpected Universe*, New York: Harcourt, Brace & World, Inc.

Sinnott, Edmund W. *The Biology of the Spirit*, New York: The Viking Press, 1955

APPENDICES

I

WISDOM OF THE AGES

The selections below represent the ancient and modern wisdom of mystics, theologians, educators, scientists and men that had a glimpse of the Infinite Light.

KNOW THYSELF

People should think less about what they ought to do and more about what they ought to be. If only their being were good, their works would shine forth brightly.
>—Meister Johannes Eckhart, 1260–1327,
>German scholar, mystic

One must be able to strip oneself of all self-deception, to see oneself naked to one's own eyes before one can come to terms with the elements of oneself and know who one really is.
>—Frances G. Wickes, 1882–,
>American psychotherapist

In other living creatures ignorance of self is nature; in man it is vice.
>—Boethius, 480(?)–524(?),
>Roman philosopher

Cleanse your own heart, cast out from your mind pain, fear, envy, ill will, avarice, cowardice, passion uncontrolled. These things you cannot cast out unless you look to God alone; on him alone set your thoughts, and consecrate yourself to his commands. If you wish for anything else, with groaning and sorrow you will follow what is stronger than you, ever seeking peace outside you, and never able to be at peace; for you seek it where it is not, and refuse to seek it where it is.

—Epictetus, A.D. 60–120,
Greek philosopher

Contemplation is a perception of God or of divine things; simple, free, penetrating, certain, proceeding from love and tending to Love.

—Louis Lallemant, 1587–1635

The difference between a good and a bad man does not lie in this, that the one wills that which is good and the other does not, but solely in this, that the one concurs with the living inspiring spirit of God within him, and the other resists it, and can be chargeable with evil only because he resists it.

—William Law, 1686–1761,
English clergyman, mystic

A man has many skins in himself, covering the depth of his heart. Man knows so many things; he does not know himself. Why, thirty or forty skins or hides, just like on an ox's or a bear's, so thick and hard, cover the soul. Go into your own ground and learn to know yourself there.

—Meister Johannes Eckhart

If the doors of perception were cleansed, everything would appear to man as it is, infinite.

For man has closed himself up, till he sees all things thro' narrow chinks in his cavern.

—William Blake, 1757–1827,
English poet, artist, mystic

By false desires and false thoughts man has built up for himself a false universe: as a mollusc, by the deliberate and persistent absorption of lime and rejection of all else, can build up for itself a hard shell which shuts it from the external world, and only represents in a distorted and unrecognizable form the ocean from which it was obtained. This hard and wholly unnutritious shell, this one-sided secretion of the surface-consciousness, makes as it were a little cave of illusion for each separate soul.

—Evelyn Underhill, 1875–1944,
English writer, mystic

Every thoughtful person who has ever considered the matter realizes that the doctors are right when they tell us that resentment, hate, grudge, ill will, jealousy, vindictiveness, are attitudes which produce ill-health. Have a fit of anger and experience for yourself that sinking feeling in the pit of your stomach, that sense of stomach sickness. Chemical reactions in the body are set up by emotional outbursts that result in feelings of ill-health. Should these be continued either violently or in a simmering state over a period of time, the general condition of the body will deteriorate.

—Norman Vincent Peale, 1898–   ,
American preacher

It is foolish to seek for God outside of oneself. This will result either in idolatry or in skepticism.

—Toyohiko Kagawa, 1888–1960,
Japanese social reformer and evangelist

All the great works and wonders that God has ever wrought . . . or even God Himself with all His goodness, can never make me blessed, but only insofar as they exist and are done and loved, known, tasted, and felt within me.

—*Theologia Germanica,* 1497

GOD

I am the holy Spirit of inspiration within thee, I am thy power to fulfill it.

—Anonymous

God is the natural appellation, for us Christians at least, for the supreme reality, so I will call this higher part of the universe by the name of God. We and God have business with each other; and in opening ourselves to his influence our deepest destiny is fulfilled. The universe, at those parts of it which our personal being constitutes, takes a turn genuinely for the worse or for the better in proportion as each one of us fulfills or evades God's demands.

—William James, 1842–1910,
American philosopher

LOVE

Love is infallible; it has no errors, for all errors are the want of love.

—William Law, 1686–1761,
English clergyman, mystic

Never wait for fitter time or place to talk to Him. To wait till thou go to church or to thy closet is to make Him wait. He will listen as thou walkest.

—George Macdonald, 1824–1905,
Scottish novelist and poet

God forces no one, for love cannot compel, and God's service, therefore, is a thing of perfect freedom.
—Hans Denk, 1495–1527,
German mystic

To love God with all our hearts and all our souls and all our minds means that every cleavage in human existence is overcome.
—Reinhold Niebuhr, 1892–1971,
American theologian, educator, author

You are a distinct portion of the essence of God; and contain part of him in yourself. Why, then, are you ignorant of your noble birth? Why do you not consider whence you came? Why do you not remember, when you are eating, who you are who eat; and whom you feed? Do you not know that it is the Divine you feed? The Divine you exercise? You carry a God about with you, poor wretch, and know nothing of it.
—Epictetus, A.D. 60–120,
Greek philosopher

PRAY
If the heart wanders or is distracted, bring it back to the point quite gently and replace it tenderly in its Master's presence. And even if you did nothing during the whole of your hour but bring your heart back and place it again in Our Lord's presence, though it went away every time you brought it back, your hour would be very well employed.
—St. Francis de Sales, 1567–1622,
French Archbishop of Geneva

Our safety does not lie in the present perfection of

our knowledge of the will of God, but in our sincerity in obeying the light we have, and in seeking for more.

—Edward Worsdell, 1853–1908,
English teacher

God is bound to act, to pour Himself into thee as soon as He shall find thee ready.

—Meister Johannes Eckhart

God wants only one thing in the whole world, the thing which it needs; . . . that thing is to find the innermost part of the noble spirit of man clean and ready for Him to accomplish the divine purpose therein. He has all power in heaven and earth, but the power to do His work in man against man's will, He has not got.

—Johann Tauler, 1304(?)–1361,
German friar-preacher

But open your eyes and the world is full of God.

—Jacob Boehme, 1575–1624,
German mystic

The right relation between prayer and conduct is not that conduct is supremely important and prayer may help it, but that prayer is supremely important and conduct tests it.

—William Temple, 1881–1944,
Archbishop of Canterbury

Immediately you awake set your first thought on God. Keep your mind on him for a few seconds. Do not think of him subjectively, as to your relation to him, your failures, your sins, or your needs, but rather objectively. Let your whole self become conscious of him. Think of him as shining beauty, radiant joy, creative

power, all-pervading love, perfect understanding, purity, and serenity. This need only take a moment or two
once the habit has been formed, but it is of inestimable
importance. It sets the tone for the whole day. . . .

One's waking mood tends to correspond to the state
of mind in which one falls asleep. If, therefore, as a result of a disturbed night or simply because of lack of
practice, this first thought of God should evade you,
look out of the window for something obviously made
by him, trees, flowers, the sky, or a wind-shaped cloud,
even a gray one, and ponder on the perfection of his
handicraft. . . .

Never get into bed with a burdened or a heavy mind;
whether it be a vague oppression or a definite fear,
shame or remorse, anger or hate, get rid of the evil thing
before you lie down to sleep. Night is a holy time, a
time of renewing and refreshment. He giveth to his beloved while they sleep; our unconscious mind is active
during our slumber. Settle down restfully to let your
mind get clear and your spirit unclogged.

—Muriel Lester, 1883–   ,
English author, social worker

Your enjoyment of the world is never right till every
morning you awake in Heaven; see yourself in your Father's palace; and look upon the skies, the earth and the
air as celestial joys; having such a reverent esteem of
all, as if you were among the Angels. The bride of a
monarch, in her husband's chamber, hath no such
causes of delight as you.

—Thomas Traherne, 1637(?)–1674,
English poet, religious writer

A frequent intercession with God, earnestly beseech-
ing him to forgive the sins of all mankind, to bless them

with his providence, enlighten them with his Spirit, and bring them to everlasting happiness, is the divinest exercise that the heart of man can be engaged in.

—William Law

Our prayer for others ought never to be: "God! give them the light Thou hast given to me!" but: "Give them all the light and truth they need for their highest development!"

—Mahatma Gandhi, 1869–1948,
Indian statesman, national leader

The seed of God is in us. Given an intelligent and hard-working farmer, it will thrive and grow up to God, whose seed it is; and accordingly its fruits will be God-nature. Pear seeds grow into pear trees, nut seeds into nut trees, and God seed into God.

—Meister Johannes Eckhart

II

MYSTICS AT PRAYER

In this section we have carefully selected prayers of mystics, sages, saints, and those whom the Light of our Creator inspired.

To derive continual benefit in your spiritual development we recommend you refer to these prayers daily.

Grant that no word may fall from me against my will unfit for the present need.

—Pericles, Athenian statesman, 495–429 B.C.

With bended knees, with hand outstretched, I pray to You, my LORD,
  O INVISIBLE BENEVOLENT SPIRIT!
  Vouchsafe to me in this hour of joy,
  All righteousness of action, all wisdom of the good
    mind,
  That I may thereby bring joy to the Soul of Creation.
    —Zoroaster, founder of ancient Persian religion,
                    sixth century B.C.

Grant me to be beautiful within, and all I have of outward things to be at peace with those within.

—Socrates, Athenian philosopher, 469–399 B.C.

O GOD, the FATHER, ORIGIN of DIVINITY, GOOD beyond all that is good, FAIR beyond all that is

fair, in WHOM is calmness, peace and concord; bring
us all back into an unity of love, which may bear some
likeness to Your sublime nature.
                              —Jacobite liturgy, third century A.D.

"Our Father in heaven,
  hallowed be your name,
  your kingdom come,
  your will be done
  on earth as it is in heaven.
  Give us today our daily bread,
  and forgive us the wrong we have done
  as we forgive those who wrong us.
  Subject us not to the trial
  but deliver us from the evil one."
                              —Jesus Christ, the Savior

Thanks be to YOU, O GOD, for everything.
              —St. Chrysostom, Greek Father of the Church
                              born in Syria, A.D. 347–409

Steer THOU the vessel of our life towards THY-
SELF, THOU tranquil Haven of all storm-tossed souls.
Show us the course wherein we should go.
              —St. Basil, Christian martyr, A.D. 329–379

May the Strength of GOD pilot us. May the Power of
GOD preserve us. May the Wisdom of GOD instruct
us. May the Way of GOD direct us.
              —St. Patrick, Christian saint, Apostle of Ireland,
                              389(?)–461(?) A.D.

ALMIGHTY GOD, we invoke THEE, the fountain
of everlasting Light, and entreat THEE to send forth

THY truth into our hearts, and to pour upon us the glory of THY Brightness.
>—Sarum breviary, fourth century, Old Sarum
>(Sorbiodunum) near Salisbury

O GOD of Unchangeable Power, let the whole world feel and see that things which were cast down are being raised up, that those which had grown old are being made new and that all things are returning to perfection.
>—Gelasian sacramentary, Gelasius, Bishop of
>Caesarea, fifth century A.D.

Grant us, O LORD, not to mind earthly things, but to love things heavenly; and even now while we are placed among things that are passing away, to cleave to those that shall abide.
>—Leonine sacramentary, fifth century, Citta Leonina,
>part of ancient Rome

O LORD, grant us to love THEE; grant that we may love those that love THEE; grant that we may do the deeds that win THY love. Make the love of THEE to be dearer than ourselves, our families, than wealth, and even than cool water.
>—Mohammed, Arabian founder of Islam,
>570–632 A.D.

Come LORD and work. Arouse us and incite. Kindle us, sweep us onwards. Be fragrant as flowers, sweet as honey. Teach us to love and to run.
>—St. Augustine, Bishop of Hippo, A.D. 354–430

LORD, teach me to know YOU, and to know myself.
>—St. Augustine

Take THOU possession of us. We give our whole selves to THEE, make known to us what THOU requirest of us, and we will accomplish it.

—St. Augustine

O ETERNAL LIGHT, shine into our hearts. O ETERNAL GOODNESS, deliver us from evil. O ETERNAL POWER, be THOU our support. ETERNAL WISDOM, scatter the darkness of our ignorance. ETERNAL PITY, have mercy upon us.

—Alcuin, archbishop, English theologian,
A.D. 735–804

I love THEE because I love; I love that I may love.

—St. Bernard, French ecclesiastic, A.D. 1091–1153

If YOU, LORD, are so good to those who seek, what shall YOUR goodness be to those who find?

—St. Bernard

Grant me fervently to desire, wisely to search out, and perfectly to fulfill all that is well-pleasing unto THEE.

—St. Thomas Aquinas, Christian priest and mystic, called "The Angelical Doctor," A.D. 1225(?)–1274

Praise be to THEE, O HIDDEN ONE and MANIFESTED ONE. Praise be to THY Glory, to THY Might, to THY Power, and to THY Great Skill.

O ALLAH, to THEE all greatness belongs. O THOU who possessest the Power and Beauty and Perfection. THOU are the Spirit of All.

Praise to THEE, O SOVEREIGN of all Monarchs; to THEE, O MASTER of all affairs; to THEE, O

CONTROLLER of all things; to THEE, RULER of all BEINGS.

THOU art free from death, free from birth and free from all limitations. O THOU ETERNAL ONE, THOU art free from all conditions, pure from all things. O ALLAH, THOU art the GOD of Souls on earth; THOU art the LORD of Hosts in the Heavens.

—Sufi invocation (Sufism, a system of Mohammedan mysticism, developed in Persia)

O LORD, I gasp in my desire for THEE, yet can I not consume THEE. The more I eat—the fiercer is my hunger; the more I drink—the greater is my thirst. I follow after that which flieth from me, and as I follow, my desire groweth greater.

—Jan van Ruysbroeck

Grant me, O LORD, heavenly wisdom, that I may learn above all things to seek and to find THEE; above all things to relish and to love THEE; and to think of all other things as being what indeed they are, at the disposal of THY wisdom.

—Thomas à Kempis, Christian mystic,
A.D. 1380–1471

LORD, we pray not for tranquillity, nor that our tribulations may cease; we pray for THY Spirit and THY love that THOU grant us strength and grace to overcome adversity.

—Girolamo Savonarola, Christian martyr,
A.D. 1452–1498

We are forced, O FATHER, to seek THEE daily, and THOU offerest THYSELF daily to be found; when-

soever we seek THEE we find THEE, in the house, in the fields, in the Temple, and in the highway.
　　　　　　　　—John Norden, sixteenth-century mystic

Defend me, O GOD, from myself.
　　　　　　　—Sir Thomas Browne, English philosopher,
　　　　　　　　　　　　　　　　A.D. 1605–1682

O give me grace to see YOUR face and be a constant mirror of ETERNITY.
　　　　　　　　　　　　　　　—Thomas Traherne

LORD, I give YOU all.
　　　　　　　—Blaise Pascal, French philosopher and
　　　　　　　　　　　mathematician, A.D. 1623–1662

LORD, I know not what I ought to ask of THEE; THOU only knowest what I need; THOU lovest me better than I know how to love myself. O FATHER, give to THY child that which he himself knows not how to ask.
　　　　—François de Salignac Fénelon, Archbishop of
　　　　　　　　Cambrai, author, A.D. 1651–1715

ALMIGHTY GOD, grant me THY grace to be faithful in action, and not anxious about success. My only concern is to do THY will, and to lose myself in THEE when engaged in duty. It is for THEE to give my weak efforts such fruits as THOU seest fit, none, if such be THY pleasure.
　　　　　　　　—François de Salignac Fénelon

O Loving-Kindness so old and still so new, I have been too late in loving THEE.

O Lord, enlarge the chambers of my heart that I may find room for THY love.

Sustain me by THY Power, lest the fire of THY love consume me.

—Brother Lawrence, Christian mystic,
A.D. 1666–1691

Draw near to my heart and inflame it. Touch my uncircumcised lips with a burning coal from THINE altar, that I may not speak of THINE ardent love in a cold or feeble manner.

—Gerhard Tersteegen, poet and ascetic,
A.D. 1697–1769

O ADMIRABLE WISDOM, that circlest all eternity, receivest into THYSELF all immensity, and drawest to THYSELF all infinity; from the inexhaustible fountain of THY light, shed some ray into my soul that I may more and more love whatever tends to THY glory and honour.

—Blaise Palma, seventeenth-century mystic

O GOD, in THEE alone can our wearied souls have full satisfaction and rest, and in THY love is the highest joy. LORD, if we have THEE, we have enough.

—Melchior Ritter, seventeenth-century mystic

O LORD, let us not live to be useless.

—John Wesley, divine and founder of Methodism,
A.D. 1703–1791

Pour upon us THY Spirit of meekness and love. Annihilate selfhood in us. Be THOU all our life.

—William Blake

I am born to serve THEE, to be THINE, to be THY instrument. Let me be THY blind instrument. I ask not to see, ask not to know; I ask simply to be used.

—John Henry Newman, English cardinal and author,
A.D. 1801–1890

Grant us grace from rest from all sinful deeds and thoughts, to surrender ourselves wholly unto THEE, and keep our souls still before THEE like a still lake, so that the beams of THY grace may be mirrored therein, and may kindle in our hearts the glow of faith and love and prayer.

—Collect from the eighteenth century

If THOU speakest not, I will fill my heart with THY silence and endure it. I will keep still and wait like the night with starry vigil and its head bent low with patience. The morning will surely come, the darkness will vanish, and THY voice pour down in golden streams, breaking through the sky.

—Rabindranath Tagore, Bengali poet and mysic,
A.D. 1861–1941

Dear GOD and FATHER of us all, forgive our faith in cruel lies; forgive the blindness that denies; forgive THY creature when he takes, for the all-perfect Love THOU art, some grim creation of his heart.

—John Greenleaf Whittier, American poet,
A.D. 1807–1892

They who never ask anything but simply love, THOU in their heart abidest for ever, for this is THY very home.

—Hindu prayer

Out of the unreal, lead me to the Real.
Out of the Darkness, lead me into the Light.
Out of Death, lead me to Deathlessness.

—Hindu prayer

Grant, GOD, protection
And in protection, strength
And in strength, understanding
And in understanding, knowledge
And in knowledge, the knowledge of the just,
And in the knowledge of the just, the love of it,
And in the love of it, the love of all existences.
And in the love of all existences, the love of GOD,
GOD and all GOODNESS.

—Gorsedd prayer

O GOD, I thank THEE for all the joy I have had in life.

—Earl Brihtnoth of the Northmen, 991–(?) A.D.

O GOD, THINE is the kingdom, the power and the Glory, for ever and ever. Amen

—Sister E. T. Cawdry, African mystic

For health, prosperity and happiness
   To THEE I pray,
But most of all a smile to greet
   The newborn day.

—Beatrice Colony, author

Let not our sins be a cloud between THEE and us.

—John Colet, Dean of St. Paul's, London, mystic,
A.D. 1467–1519

THY glory alone, O GOD, be the end of all that we say;

Let it shine in every deed, let it kindle the prayers
    that I pray;
Let it burn in my innermost soul till the shadow of
    self pass away,
And the light of THY glory, O GOD, be unveiled in
    the dawning of day.

                  —F. W. Scott, English writer

Behold THY creature; do with me what THOU wilt.
I have nothing, my GOD, that holds me back. I am
THINE alone.

                  —Scupoli, mystic

Tomorrow
I am content to leave with him
Who gives today
For today the sun smiles
And the earth responds,
And a twinkling, singing sea
Forms lacy patterns on the sand.
O, GOD,
I am grateful
For this day!
    —E. C. Wilson, American writer and philosopher

GOD be merciful to me, a fool.
  —Edward Rowland Sill, American poet and author,
                      A.D. 1841–1887

May it be Thy will, O God, that we return to Thee
in perfect penitence, so that we may not be ashamed
to meet our fathers in the life to come.

                  —Talmud

SELECTED BIBLIOGRAPHY

The listing below represents a basic core of books published in English on prayer and fasting. Especially recommended books on prayer are marked with an asterisk.

Books on Prayer:

* Allen, Charles L., *All Things Are Possible Through Prayer*, 1958

* Armstrong, H. Parr, *Living in the Currents of God*, 1962

Austin, Mary, *Can Prayer Be Answered?* 1934

Baillie, John, *A Diary of Private Prayer*, 1950

Baker, F. Augustine, *Holy Wisdom, or Directions for the Prayer of Contemplation*, N.D.

Banks, J. B., *The Master and the Disciple—Devotional Reading*, 1954

Barry, J. G. H., *On Prayer to the Dead*, 1922

Bauman, Edward W., *Intercessory Prayer*, 1958

Belden, Alfred, *The Practice of Prayer*, N.D.

Boggis, R. J. E., *Praying for the Dead*, 1913

Bro, H. H., *Dreams in the Life of Prayer, The Approach of Edgar Cayce*, 1970

Bro, M., *More Than We Are*, 1965

Campbell, James H., *The Place of Prayer in the Christian Religion*

Carrel, Alexis, *Prayer*, 1949

Casteel, John H., *Renewal in Retreats*, 1959

Clark, Glenn, *I Will Lift Up Mine Eyes*, N.D.

Clarke, James Freeman, *The Christian Doctrine of Prayer*

Dallas, Helen Alex, Ed., *Communion and Fellowship (Aids to the Bereaved)*, 1921

Day, Albert E., *An Autobiography of Prayer*, 1952

Fillmore, Charles and Cora, *Teach Us to Pray*, 1941

* Fillmore, L., *The Prayer Way to Find Health, Wealth, and Happiness*, 1964

Fluck, D., *Better Health Through Prayer*, N.D.

Forsythe and Greenwell, *The Power of Prayer*,

Fosdick, Harry Emerson, *The Meaning of Prayer*, 1915

Freer, Harold, *God Meets Us Where We Are*, 1967

Freer and Hall, *Two or Three Together: A Manual for Prayer Groups*, 1954

* French, R.M., *The Way of a Pilgrim*, 1960

Frost, B., *The Art of Mental Prayer*, 1931

Gordon, S. D., *Quiet Talks on Prayer*, 1967

Grou, J. N., *How to Pray*, 1955

Hanky, P., *Signposts on the Christian Way*, 1962

Harkness, G., *Prayer and the Common Life*, 1948

Heard, Gerald, *Preface to Prayer*, 1944

Herman, E., *Creative Prayer*, N.D.

Herrman, Wilhelm, *Communion With God*

Ikin, A. Graham, *Life, Faith and Prayer*, 1954

Jones, Rufus, M., *The Double Search*

Kelly, T. R., *Testament of Devotion*, 1941

Lake, Alexander, *Your Prayers Are Always Answered*, 1956

* Laubach, F. C., *Prayer, The Mightiest Force in the World*, 1946

Leen, Edward, *Progress Through Mental Prayer*, 1935

* Loehr, Franklin, *The Power of Prayer on Plants*, 1959

* Mack, Gwynne, *Talking With God: The Healing Power of Prayer*, 1961

Maclachlan, L., *Common Sense About Prayer*, 1962

⸻, *How to Pray for Healing*, 1963

⸻, *Intelligent Prayer*, 1946

⸻, *The Teaching of Jesus on Prayer*, 1952

⸻, *Twenty-One Steps to Positive Prayer*, 1965

Magee, John, *Reality and Prayer*, 1957

Magee, Raymond, *Call to Adventure—The Retreat as Religious Experience,* 1967

Mann, Stella, *Change Your Life Through Prayer,* 1955

————, *How to Live in the Circle of Prayer,* 1959

Matson, Archie, *A Month With the Master,* 1958

McComb, Samuel, *Prayer, What It Is and What It Does*

McFadyen, John Edgar, *The Prayer of the Bible*

Murray, A., *With Christ in the School of Prayer,* 1885

Neville, *Prayer, The Art of Believing,* 1943

* Parker, and St. Johns, *Prayer Can Change Your Life,* 1957

Poulain, A., *The Graces of Interior Prayer,* N.D.

Rawson, F. L., *The Nature of True Prayer,* 1930

————, *Right Thinking, the Basis of True Prayer,* 1919

Russell, A. J., *God Calling,* 1948

Sherman, Harold, *How to Use the Power of Prayer,* 1958

* Shoemaker, H., *The Secret of Effective Prayer*

* Steere, Douglas, *Dimensions of Prayer,* 1962

————, *Prayer and Worship,* 1938

Strong, Anna Louise, *The Psychology of Prayer*

Swetenham, L., *Conquering Prayer*

Trumbull, H. Clay, *Prayer, Its Nature and Scope*

Weatherhead, L. D., *A Private House of Prayer,* 1958

Winslow, Jack C., *When I Awake,* 1938

Wuellner, F., *Prayer and the Living Christ*

Books on Fasting:

Bragg, Paul C., *The Miracle of Fasting,* 1972

Brown, Harold R., *The Fast Way to Health and Vigor,* 1961

Carrel, Alexis, *Man, the Unknown,* 1932

Carrington, Hereward, *Fasting for Health and Long Life,* 1953

Carrington, *Vitality, Fasting and Nutrition* 1908

Ehret, Arnold, *Rational Fasting,*

Hazzard, Linda B., *Scientific Fasting,* 1963

Langfield, Herbert S., "On the Psychophysiology of a Prolonged Fast"; *Psychological Monographs,* Volume XVI, No. 5; Harvard University: July, 1914

MacFadden, Bernarr A., *Fasting for Health,* 1934

Prince, Derek, *Restoration Through Fasting,*

Shelton, Herbert M., *Fasting Can Save Your Life*, 1964
Sinclair, Upton, *The Fasting Cure*,
Wallis, Arthur, *A Spiritual and Practical Guide to Fasting*, 1972

AUTHOR INDEX